Ruth Benedict

Leaders of Modern Anthropology Series

Charles Wagley, GENERAL EDITOR

RUTH BENEDICT

by Margaret Mead

Columbia University Press

1974 NEW YORK AND LONDON

Library of Congress Cataloging in Publication Data

Mead, Margaret, 1901–
    Ruth Benedict.

    (Leaders of modern anthropology series)
    Bibliography: p.
    1. Benedict, Ruth (Fulton) 1887–1948.
2. Ethnology.   I. Series.
GN21.B45M42 1974   301.2′092′4 [B]   74–6400
ISBN 0–231–03519–5
ISBN 0–231–03520–9 (pbk.)

Preface

Blackstone Studios

❖ This brief biography differs in several respects from other biographics in this series. My own earlier professional life almost exactly paralleled Ruth Benedict's in time; although she was fifteen years my senior, she entered anthropology only three years before I did. Throughout her professional life we worked together. We took over responsibilities for each other's students when one or the other was absent and we corresponded frequently to and from the field.

As her literary executor I have had access to all her papers, which were organized by her friend, Marie E. Eichelberger, and were deposited in the Vassar College Library. Because I have had access to so many letters and private journals, I have been able to tell much of the story of her life in her own words. Moreover, I have already brought together a great deal of this material in a much more lengthy book about her, *An Anthropologist at Work: Writings of Ruth Benedict*, published in 1959. This book is in print and can be consulted whenever the reader wishes to follow up some point in greater detail. In the present volume I have made a somewhat different selection of Ruth Benedict's papers with a view to the interests of contemporary readers.

NEW YORK   MARGARET MEAD
June 1974   THE AMERICAN MUSEUM OF NATURAL HISTORY

Acknowledgments

✤ For permission to reproduce previously published materials grateful acknowledgment is made to Charles Scribner's Sons for a passage from *Franz Boas: The Science of Man in the Making* by Melville J. Herskovits, copyright 1953; to the University of Chicago Press for material from *The Study of Culture at a Distance* edited by Margaret Mead and Rhoda Metraux, copyright 1953; to the Regents of the University of California and the California University Press for a passage from *More Mohave Myths* by Alfred L. Kroeber, copyright 1972; and to the *University of Toronto Quarterly* for a passage from "Ruth Benedict: Apollonian and Dionesian" by Victor Barnouw (1948).

For permission to reproduce previously published work by Ruth Benedict grateful acknowledgment is made also to the *American Anthropologist* for a passage from "A Brief Sketch of Serrano Culture" (1924), "Configurations of Culture in North America" (1932) and "Anthropology and the Humanities" (1948); to the *Atlantic Monthly* for "Primitive Freedom," copyright © 1942, R 1970 by the Atlantic Monthly Company, Boston, Mass.; to the Columbia University Press for portions of the introduction to *Zuni Mythology*, copyright 1935; to Houghton Mifflin Company and Routledge & Kegan Paul, Ltd., for passages from *Patterns of Culture*, copyright 1934 by Ruth Benedict and to Houghton Mifflin Company for extensive passages by Ruth Benedict and others from *An*

Acknowledgments

Anthropologist at Work: Writings of Ruth Benedict by Margaret Mead, copyright 1959 by Margaret Mead, and for portions of two chapters from *The Chrysanthemum and the Sword,* copyright 1946 by Ruth Benedict; to the *Journal of General Psychology* for a passage from "Anthropology and the Abnormal" (1934); to the Macmillan Publishing Company for "Magic" in the *Encyclopedia of the Social Sciences* edited by Edwin R. A. Seligman and others, copyright by the Macmillan Company, 1933; to *The Nation* for the poem "Eucharist" by "Anne Singleton" (1928); to The New York Academy of Sciences for "The Study of Cultural Patterns in European Nations," published in *Transactions* (1946); and to the Wenner-Gren Foundation for Anthropological Research (Viking Fund) for the poem "Myth," from *Ruth Benedict: A Memorial* (1948).

Contents

Ruth Benedict

Ruth Benedict, a Humanist in Anthropology

Ruth Fulton Benedict was one of the first women to attain major stature as a social scientist. When she entered anthropology in 1919, it was still an esoteric science. By 1948, when she died, an awareness of the relativity of cultural values and some grasp of the significance of the study of cultures, primitive and modern, extended far beyond anthropology. She herself played a decisive part in bringing about this transformation.

Patterns of Culture is her best known work.[1] For more than a generation it has served not only as an introduction to anthropology but also as a guide to students in many fields who have sought for an approach to an unfolding world. Now, forty years after the book's publication, it is as alive as when it was written, for in it Ruth Benedict addressed herself to a problem that is poignantly contemporary: How is the diversity of the human search for meaning to be understood? Her exposition, scholarly in depth and infused with aesthetic appreciation in the best tradition of English literature, broke through the formal boundaries of a single social science to clarify our understanding of the human estate.

[1] PUBLISHED IN 1934, *Patterns of Culture* has been translated into twelve other languages and, in English alone, has sold some 1.6 million copies.

As a young woman, long before she discovered anthropology, Ruth Benedict wrote in her journal:

> *The trouble with life isn't that there is no answer, it's that there are so many answers. There's the answer of Christ and of Buddha, of Thomas à Kempis and of Elbert Hubbard, of Browning, Keats and of Spinoza, of Thoreau and of Walt Whitman, of Kant and of Theodore Roosevelt. By turns their answers fit my needs. And yet, because I am I and not any one of them, they can none of them be completely mine.* (AAW: 126) [2]

This theme of her own personal search for meaning and for an under-standing of the individual's place within his own culture and society illu-minates all of Ruth Benedict's writings, from her earliest extant journal and her sketch of the life of Mary Wollstonecraft ([1917] AAW: 491–519). At the end of this short biography she wrote:

> *In the National Portrait Gallery hangs a picture of Mary Wollstonecraft, a picture of her as she was a few scant months before her death. I remember the child I was when I saw it first, haunted by the terror of youth before experience. I wanted so desperately to know how other women had saved their souls alive. And the woman in the little frame arrested me, this woman with the auburn hair, and the sad, steady, light-brown eyes, and the gallant poise of the head. She had saved her soul alive; it looked out from her steady eyes unafraid. The price, too, that life had demanded of her was written ineradicably there. But to me, then, standing before her picture, even that costly payment was a guarantee, a promise. For I knew that in those days when she sat for that picture, she was content. And in the light of that content, I still spell out her life.* (AAW: 519)

I met Ruth Benedict in the autumn of 1922, when I was a senior at Barnard College. She had just completed her graduate studies under Franz Boas at Columbia University and, as his assistant at Barnard Col-

---

[2] PUBLISHED IN *An Anthropologist at Work: Writings of Ruth Benedict*, by Margaret Mead (1959). For the sake of brevity this work will be referred to here as AAW.

lege for one year, she was taking groups of us to the American Museum of Natural History.

At this time her beauty, which had been conspicuous in her girlhood and was to become legendary in later years, was completely in eclipse. We saw her as a very shy, almost distrait, middle-aged woman whose fine, mouse-colored hair never stayed quite pinned up. Week after week she wore a very prosaic hat and the same drab dress. Men wore the same clothes every day, she said. Why shouldn't a woman, also? She stammered a little when she talked with us and sometimes blushed scarlet. On one occasion when she was speaking about Plains Indian cultures, as we were gathered around a miniature model of the Sun Dance, I asked a detailed question. She replied hurriedly, in a manner which I at first perceived as brushing me aside, that she would give me something later. What troubled her was diffidence about mentioning her own work, as I realized when the next week she gave me the small, bright blue reprint of her first publication, "The Vision in Plains Culture" (1922).

In spite of her shyness, Ruth Benedict's enthusiasm for the anthropological world she had so recently entered and her delight in the detail of primitive ritual and poetry—which I soon discovered was joined with a deep interest in modern poetry—captivated all of us. The intensity of her interest, combined with the magnificent clarity of Boas' teaching, made anthropology, as such, something of a revelation to me. I was the child of social scientists and the basic ideas of the independence of race, language, and culture, as well as the importance of the comparative method, were already familiar to me. What was new to me was the emphasis on the intricate details of primitive cultures, a kind of detail of which there was no hint in the work of the comparative socioeconomists—Veblen, Paton, and Caseby—who had been my parents' teachers. Following Ruth Benedict's suggestions I spent long evenings when I was baby-sitting memorizing Australian and Toda kinship systems or copying out Northwest Coast designs until I had the feel of those marvelously dissected sharks and eagles in my fingertips.

She brought home to us also the desperate urgency of doing anthropological field work before the last precious and irretrievable memories of traditional American Indian cultures were carried to the grave. She herself had done her first field work in the summer of 1922, among the

3

Morongo Valley Serrano, one of the Shoshonean groups of southern California. This was the situation she found, as she described it in "A Brief Sketch of Serrano Culture" (1924):

> *Such information as may be gathered among the Serrano today is almost entirely exoteric. No old shaman (hümtc) or priest (paha) survives. The annual fiesta is still kept up in a modified form, and until a few years ago the Morongo Reservation Serrano depended on a sha-man of the desert Cahuilla for some of the old dances and shamanistic performances. A great deal of the old meaning, both in social organi-zation and in religious practices, is undoubtedly lost. It is largely by guesswork that they can give the meaning of any of the ceremonial songs; and any religious connotation in such practices as rock-painting, for instance, is now unknown. It must therefore remain an open ques-tion in many cases, as for instance the universal animal designations of all local groups, whether the absence of any esoteric interpretations today is the reflection of an old Serrano trait, or is due to a fading of the old traditions. (pp. 366–68)*

Much of what working within a vanishing culture meant to a field-worker was conveyed only very inarticulately to students like ourselves, who knew almost nothing about what field work might consist of or how it was carried out. Yet Ruth Benedict made the old men and women who were her informants very real to us and endowed them with the same poi-gnancy that, many years later, came through so clearly in her evocation of the figure of speech used by a chief of the Digger Indians:

> *"In the beginning," he said, "God gave to every people a cup, a cup of clay, and from this cup they drank their life." I do not know whether the figure occurred in some traditional ritual of his people that I never found, or whether it was his own imagery. . . . At any rate, in the mind of this humble Indian the figure of speech was clear and full of meaning. "They all dipped in the water," he continued, "but their cups were different. Our cup is broken now. It has passed away." (1934b: 21–22)*

4

As she talked with us, she made the breakdown and disappearance of the traditional culture vivid and irreparable. But she was not sentimental about the possibility of preserving Indian societies or romantic about Indians who had been disinherited. She was protected from sentimentality by her own maturity and this, in turn, protected us.

THE EARLY YEARS

She was born Ruth Fulton, on June 5, 1887, in a farming community in the Shenango Valley in northern New York State, where both her paternal and her maternal grandparents lived. Her mother, Beatrice Shattuck, had studied at Vassar College. Her father, Frederick S. Fulton, was a brilliant young surgeon with a promising career in research in New York. While Ruth was still a baby, her father fell ill of an obscure, undiagnosed disease. The young family returned to live on the Shattuck farm where Ruth's only sister, Margery, was born a few weeks before their father's death in March 1889.

Ruth grew up with her maternal grandfather's farm as the background of her life. When she was five, her mother—who was unusually independent for her day—began teaching in the nearby town of Norwich and soon thereafter took the two children to live first in St. Joseph, Missouri, then in Owatonna, Minnesota, and finally in Buffalo, New York, in order to make her living as a teacher and later as a librarian. But the Shattuck farm, to which they returned each summer and where a favorite spinster aunt lived in later years, remained home to Ruth for all her life.

Her memories of her childhood as she wrote about them, in 1935, in a fragmentary autobiography stress her sense of alienation. "Happiness," she wrote, "was a world I lived in all by myself, and for precious moments" (AAW: 100). She was repelled by her mother's persistent, grieving widowhood and she herself was given to violent, seizure-like tantrums which she traced back to a traumatic scene beside her father's coffin, where her mother passionately adjured her to remember her father's face. Very early in life she was partially deafened by illness, but for a long time this was not recognized and she was chided for being unresponsive—in contrast to her sunny-tempered, pretty, and less complicated younger sister, Margery.

5

RUTH AND
MARGERY FULTON
AS CHILDREN.

She remembered the world at the farm with deep joy in the landscape, which she had peopled with imaginary companions. But in later years she often spoke of how she had come to feel, very early, that there was little in common between the beliefs of her family and neighbors and her own passionate wondering about life, which she soon learned to keep to herself. The Bible, rigidly adhered to by her firmly fundamentalist relatives, became the background of her daydreams, but her feeling about it was so different from that of her family that her delight in the Bible was still another source of alienation. In this way she laid the basis of an inner life that could be her own as long as she never told anyone about it. Long afterward she commented to a friend: "This is a dangerous thing for a child to learn." For years her inner life found expression only in the journals she kept intermittently and, later, in poetry, which she began to publish under various pseudonyms of which one, Anne Singleton, eventually became known. The two aspects of her life—her private, inner life and the part she acknowledged to others—began to merge only when at last she came into anthropology and met anthropologists who were also interested in poetry.

Although the years while she and her sister were growing up were difficult because of the stringent economies necessary to make ends meet, she herself was indifferent to material possessions. However, her early experience of deprivation—in Buffalo this meant being poorer than any of her classmates—made her keenly sympathetic with the plight of her students in the Depression years, when she gave every penny she could spare from a meager salary to eke out the miserable funds available for writing up their field work. But, in fact, the financial deprivation of her childhood came about through her father's premature death. It was deprivation against a solid background of family security—on the farm with her grandfather, whom she deeply trusted, and in relation to aunts and uncles and cousins, all of whom were moderately well off.

Her accounts of the years in Minnesota and Buffalo before she and Margery went to Vassar, in 1905, centered on her early struggles to understand the life around her, to master her uncontrollable tantrums, to maintain a cool and tearless exterior while experiencing intense inner turmoil, and to seek for moments of delight in maple buds "scarlet on the sky." In high school she began to write. This she regarded as in some way a compensation for the fact that, unlike her sister, she was not handy and found housework and making her own clothes "terribly trying." Later in life she did all chores quickly and competently, but absentmindedly and with the conviction that *not* everything that was worth doing was worth doing well.

At college, where she majored in English literature, she was still solitary and strangely attractive to other lonely people. When she graduated in 1909, she was invited to accompany two of her classmates on a carefully chaperoned trip to Europe. Then after a year during which she lived with her mother in Buffalo and worked for the Charity Organization Society, she left home—as her mother had—to begin teaching. For one year, 1911–1912, she taught in the Westlake School for Girls in Los Angeles and for the next two years, 1912–1914, in the Orton School for Girls in Pasadena. Here she was near Margery, who had married Robert Freeman, a young, progressive minister. In the childless years to come it was Margery's home, full of children, that gave Ruth a sense of having a family. And it was in making baby clothes for Margery's children that she developed pleasure in doing occasional pieces of fine needlework.

This period of teaching in girls' schools was the time when she came face to face with her life as a woman. Although she had met the man she later married—he was the brother of a Vassar classmate—she had no idea then that she would marry him. Life in a girls' school, with its endless round of chaperoning students and supervising their study hours, depressed her, and she was preoccupied by her feeling that women primarily want to love and be loved. In October 1912, she wrote in her journal:

> *So much of the trouble is because I am a woman. To me it seems a very terrible thing to be a woman. There is one crown which perhaps is worth it all—a great love, a quiet home, and children. We all know that is all that is worth while, and yet we must peg away, showing off our wares on the market if we have money, or manufacturing careers for ourselves if we haven't. We have not the motive to prepare ourselves for a "life-work" of teaching, of social work—we know that we would lay it down with hallelujah in the height of our success, to make a home for the right man.*
>
> *And all the time in the background of our consciousness rings the warning that perhaps the right man will never come. A great love is given to very few. Perhaps this make-shift time filler of a job is our life work after all.* (AAW: 120)

The thought of the future, an unchanging future, obsessed her, and she wrote: "Perhaps my trouble comes from thinking of the end as my *present* self, not as a possible and very different future self" (AAW: 122). And watching the spinsters around her, she felt that for many women finding a "great love" was unlikely. She daydreamed of exchanging teaching for "a garden of hollyhocks and pansies against the old apple trees and lilacs" at her grandfather's farm (AAW: 127).

At the end of the school year she talked about her doubts with the headmistress of the Orton School, who told her: " 'We narrow our interests until we grow fossilized, as—as I am. And then we have to make our teaching fill our lives. We have to, to live. I want you to have many in-

THE SHATTUCK FARM AT NORWICH, NEW YORK, ABOUT 1900.
Left to right: RUTH'S AUNT, MYRA F. SHATTUCK, GRANDPA AND GRANDMA SHATTUCK.

terests. You have much to expect of life' " (AAW: 128). Temporarily reassured, she agreed to come back to the school for another year.

But within weeks of her return to the Shattuck farm for the summer, she wrote in her journal:

> *Yes, I am coming back to the farm. I'll make something off the garden and the orchard—perhaps in time it will be a prosperous business. And except for my four months' vacation in the winter, I shall not need much money. I'm coming primarily because I want to—because I can't believe that joyless life is significant life.* (AAW: 128)

The idea of farming tasks presented no difficulties. She was a tall, strong woman with large, capable hands. She enjoyed physical activities—walking and vigorous swimming—and sometimes sought catharsis in chopping up logs for firewood.

Yet for her, farming—like teaching—was only a means. What was essential, she wrote, was something else:

> *to find a way of living not utterly incongruous with certain passionate ideals: to attain to a zest for life, an enthusiasm for the adventure which will forever deliver me from my shame of cowardice, to master an attitude toward life which will somehow bind together these episodes of experience into something that may conceivably be called life.* (AAW: 128–29)

The farm would give her "the out-door life I love, the leisure, the home-life" (AAW: 129). Still she worried:

> *There is only one argument that troubles me. It is the fear of being a quitter, of having run away from the fight for my own private enjoyment. The faith this world needs is the faith that can hold its own in the rub and irritating contact of the world. I plan large work among the farmers and their children to salve my conscience. But I do not know——.* (AAW: 129)

10

A month after this decision, in August 1913, she fell in love with Stanley Benedict and promised to marry him. Then she wrote in her journal:

> *And so the whole world changed. Is it not awesome—wonderful beyond expression? Every day I have grown surer, happier. Nothing in all my life would be worth setting over against our Sunday afternoon drive through Lyon Brook or our last afternoon together on the towpath.*
>
> *We turn in our sleep and groan because we are parasites—we women—because we produce nothing, say nothing, find our whole world in the love of a man.—For shame! We are become the veriest Philistines—in this matter of woman's sphere. I suppose it is too soon to expect us to achieve perspective on the problem of woman's rights—but surely there is no other problem of human existence where we would be childish enough to believe in the finality of our little mathematical calculations of "done" or "not done." But here in the one supremely complicated relation of man and woman which involves the perpetual interchange of all that is most difficult to be reckoned—here we thrust in "the world's coarse thumb and finger," here we say "to the eyes of the public shalt thou justify thy existence." —Oh no! do we care whether Beatrice formed clubs, or wrote a sonnet? In the quiet self-fulfilling love of Wordsworth's home, do we ask that Mary Wordsworth should have achieved individual self-expression? In general,—a woman has one supreme power—to love. If we are to arrive at any blytheness in facing life, we must have faith to believe that it is in exercising this gift, in living it out to its fullest that she achieves herself, that she "justifies her existence."* (AAW: 130)

Ruth Fulton was speaking here as a woman newly in love. But her words have a premonitory ring. Essentially she was expressing what so many young people of both sexes half a century later have come to believe—that life is justified by the intensity of immediate experience and love.

In the autumn she returned, after all, to California and taught one more year at the Orton School. Then, in the summer of 1914, she married Stanley Benedict. At this time he was beginning a long and distinguished career as a biochemist at Cornell Medical College in New York City. During the first years of their marriage they lived in the Long Island suburb of Douglas Manor. By 1922 she came to think of suburban life as worse than the worst slums, more stultifying and soul-destroying.

STANLEY R. BENEDICT,
AT ABOUT THE TIME OF HIS
MARRIAGE TO RUTH FULTON IN 1914.

Charles H. Beal

RUTH FULTON,
THE CALIFORNIA YEARS.

But describing it to me, she quickly added, "Not that I am in favor of slums!"

At first, however, she gloried in her newfound leisure. She wrote: "The winter is before me to accomplish anything I wish. I have difficulty only in concentrating on something. . . . " (AAW: 132). "For amusement" she thought of writing "chemical detective" stories for which Stanley would supply the plots and "social work" stories based on her year's work in Buffalo. She wanted to read Shakespeare and Goethe. She wanted to "keep a book full of notes." But her pet scheme was to

steep myself in the lives of restless and highly enslaved women of past generations and write a series of biographical papers from the standpoint of the "new woman." My conclusion so far as I see it now is that there is nothing "new" about the whole thing except the phraseology and the more independent economic standing of recent times—that the restlessness and groping are inherent in the nature of women and this generation can outdo the others long since past only in the frankness with which it acts upon these; that nature lays a compelling and very distressing hand upon woman, and she struggles in vain who tries to deny it or escape it,—life loves the little irony of proving it upon the very woman who has denied it; she can only hope for success by working according to Nature's preconceptions of her make-up—not against them. (AAW: 132–33)

This was a far cry from her later theoretical understanding of the myriad ways in which culture modifies human demands on men and women, while still presenting difficulties to those born in a particular culture, whose temperament—rather than whose sex—provides an intractable obstacle to the achievement of their aspirations.

In 1915 war was raging in Europe. But what gripped Ruth Benedict at this time was the intensity of her own inner turmoil. She longed for the child that did not come, but she also realized that having a child would not wholly meet her urgent need. She wrote in her journal:

There is no one of our radiant faiths that seems more surely planted and reared in us by a mocking Master of the Revels than that which shines out from all of us in our radiant faith in "our children."— The dreams that slipped from us like the sand in the hour glass, the task we laid aside to give them birth and rearing,—all this they shall carve in the enduring stone of their achievements— The master stroke of the irony, the stabbing hurt of it, is that it is all so noble and self-less a dream; it is truly, "that last infirmity of noble minds." (AAW: 133)

13

And she wondered:

> *And surely the world has need of my vision as well as of Char-*
> *ity Committees; it is better to grow straight than to twist myself into a*
> *doubtfully useful footstool; it is better to make the most of that deepest*
> *cry of my heart: "Oh God let me be awake—awake in my lifetime."*
> (AAW: 135)

In her search for intellectual bearings—her effort to find herself as a
person—she wrote, dissociating herself from Stanley:

> *I must have my world too, my outlet, my chance to put forth my effort.*
> *And never did desires dovetail more neatly—for I don't want a "posi-*
> *tion," heaven forbid! nor a committee chairmanship—All I want I can*
> *do here at home in my ready-to-hand leisure. The only necessity is that I*
> *should realize my purposes seriously enough and work at writing with*
> *sufficient slavishness.*
> *—If I had children or were expecting one, it would call a truce to*
> *these promptings, I suppose. But surely it would be only a truce—it*
> *would sign no permanent terms of peace with them. . . .*

> *There is no misreading of life that avenges itself so piteously on men*
> *and women as the notion that in their children they can bring to frui-*
> *tion their own seedling dreams. And it is just as unjust to the child, to*
> *be born and reared as the "creation" of his parents. He is* himself, *and*
> *it is within reason that he may be the very antithesis of them both.—*
> *No, it is wisdom in motherhood as in wifehood to have one's own indi-*
> *vidual world of effort and creation.* (AAW: 136)

Throughout this difficult period she was working on the first of her
projected biographies of "restless and highly enslaved women of past generations," the life of Mary Wollstonecraft. But a year later, in October
1916, she wrote in discouragement:

> *Again another winter. It is hard for me to look with any satis-*
> *faction on the two winters that are passed—and now another. "Mary*

Wollstonecraft" I do believe in—but will she ever be published? I doubt it, and more and more I know that I want publication. (AAW: 135)

That December she and Stanley went up to their house on Lake Winnepesaukee, where they spent every vacation. There, where she felt "strong and eager and in love with life," she tried again to make a viable plan:

> *The particular problem of this winter is how I may cut through the . . . entanglements of our order of life and make good in my writing. I would like to simplify our living . . . .—cut away the incubus of a house and coal fires and course dinners.* (AAW: 137–38)

On Christmas Day—"snowbound at the Lake"—she seemed to have reached a turning point:

> *I've pledged my word to a "business in life" now. Last night Stanley and I talked. . . .*
> *I said that for the sake of our love—our friendship, rather—I must pay my way in a job of my own. I would not, would not drift into the boredom, the pitiableness of lives like —— or ——. He said that, whatever the job, it would not hold me; nothing ever had, social work or teaching. Children might for a year or two, no more. . . .*
> *I told him he should see. My past list of jobs proved nothing: until I loved him nothing had ever seemed to me worth the effort of attaining. I could lay hold of no motive. Now I understood; I cared and cared deeply. . . . I should prove that I was no rolling stone. I should prove too that whatever I could achieve in my own life was something added to our relationship with each other.*
> *—And now I must prove my word. I must bind it to me till it is closer than breathing, nearer than hands and feet. It means that for the first time in my life, I have committed myself to the endeavor for success—success in writing. It means that before summer I shall have completed "Adventures in Womanhood"—and found a publisher for them. It means that what I can do to get them into the magazines, I will do. It means that with all the force within me, I will write, this winter.* (AAW:138–39)

In May 1917, however, she reported that all her plans had gone awry. Instead of writing she had spent the winter organizing day nurseries. "In a sense," she wrote, "I'm satisfied with the job. I've called an organization into being that's doing good work, and needed work. . . . A dozen other

RUTH BENEDICT,
EARLY MARRIED YEARS.

women are working well who otherwise wouldn't have had a niche to work in" (AAW: 142). But the dilemma remained:

The other day when I was getting up an open meeting and spending the day at the telephone, I wept because I came across a jumbled untouched verse manuscript. Yet I suppose I'd reverse the cause of tears if I were to pin my next decade to writing alone. And yet oh, I long to prove myself by writing! The best seems to die in me when I give it up. It is the self I love—not this efficient, philanthropic self. And isn't that the test? (AAW: 142)

She did, in fact, finish "Mary Wollstonecraft" in 1917, but the manuscript was rejected by Houghton Mifflin. Forty-one years later the same publisher brought it out in *An Anthropologist at Work* (1959). But this Ruth Benedict never knew.

During the whole decade beginning in 1911, when she successively tried social work and teaching and then put so much hope into her marriage to Stanley, her desperate need was to find herself—to commit herself to a way of life that had meaning for her and that drew on all her talents. Again and again, during these years her journals record her struggles and her maturing sense of what the issues were for the women of her generation who, like herself, were struggling to break the bonds of their traditional identifications. Later, when she had already found her own direction, she tried again to formulate the issues:

> *In the progress of feminism the issues have been drawn usually on some variation of parasitism vs. labor—Mrs. Gilman claimed it for the sake of woman's economic independence, Olive Schreiner for the sake of her self-fulfillment. I think conditions are rapidly falsifying these issues: the vast majority have the right to labor now—wartimes have seen to that—in the great war-game no one is exempted. And it is a necessary emancipation; without it there would be no further step. But it is only initial. Our factories are filled with women and girls, and their experience is as nothing—nothing—in their development. They get from it no sense of the dignity of associated labor, no sense of the contributive value of their product, no experience in organized self-government. It is along these lines, through trades organizations, that this pointless labor must be made a factor in the onward march of women.*
>
> *Practically all the "labor" open to the majority of women is open to the same objection; something must be done to it before it can have any value. That value can be gained quite as surely off a pay roll as on it. No, I do not believe that the modern conditions require any longer the issue of labor—paid labor vs. parasitism. . . .*
>
> *What is it then? Initiative to go after the big things of life—not freedom from somewhat; initiative for somewhat. Now for some women the big things of life include political activity and it is abundantly right*

17

that they should seek their place there. For the great majority of women, however, the big things of life are love, children, social activity according to their abilities. And in the matter of love and children there is no initiative, liberty of conscience, permitted. But it is necessary that we have some voice in the conditions under which these big things of our lives shall be realized, that we have the freedom for their achievement. The emotional part of woman's life—that part which makes her a woman—must be brought up out of the dark and allowed to put forth its best. (AAW: 145–46)

But in 1917 she had not yet found her direction. During the war years Stanley worked on problems of the biochemistry of poison gas and was himself badly gassed. This accentuated his need for isolation and his desire to spend long summers at the lake in New Hampshire. Ruth could no longer bear the trivialities of life in Douglas Manor. But after living for a year in New York, they moved even further from the city, to Bedford Hills. In this period Ruth experimented with rhythmic dancing, in which she took great pleasure. She also spent another year doing social work for the State Charities Aid Association. After that her strong sense of social responsibility took other forms.

The decisive turning point in her life came in 1919, when she went to the New School for Social Research, where she attended lectures for two years. At first this was one more attempt to fill time intelligently, for she still kept alive the hope of having a child. But during this period she finally learned that she could not have a child without undergoing a very problematic operation for which Stanley refused to give his consent. Facing empty years in a childless marriage, she recognized that she must commit herself to her "own individual world of effort and creation." Then, as she listened to the very contrasting lectures given by Alexander Goldenweiser and Elsie Clews Parsons, she discovered anthropology. Here, in this new science, was substance she could respect. Here she could use all her talents and also perhaps find answers to her most pressing personal questions: Why did she feel herself to be a stranger in contemporary America? What, for her, was ultimately worth doing?

Earlier she had written in her journal:

18

RUTH BENEDICT WITH HER SISTER'S CHILDREN.

The highest endowments do not create—they only discover. All transcendent genius has the power to make us know this as utter truth. Shakespeare, Beethoven—it is inconceivable that they have fash- ioned the works of their lives; they only saw and heard the universe that is opaque and dumb to us. When we are most profoundly moved by them, we say, not "O superb creator"—but "O how did you know! Yes it is so." Lesser men may give us a very keen pleasure through "cre- ation," as Poe does, as Stevenson does, but even they are caught at times up into that realm where they too discover the uncredited;—and then we pause in our tribute to their skill, and for the moment are sim- ply one with them in their discovery. And those moments are all their glory. (AAW: 141)

Now, as she learned what a culture is, she came to feel that it was pos- sible to view a primitive culture holistically, much as works of art are viewed in our culture—as something to be "discovered," something that was not "fashioned" but that came to be an integrated whole.

19

ANTHROPOLOGY: THE YEARS OF A GROWING COMMITMENT

In 1921, at the age of thirty-four, Ruth Benedict went to Columbia University to take a degree under Franz Boas. By the time she was prepared to take advantage of the research fellowships that were beginning to be available, she was over thirty-five and beyond the acceptable age limits. She had to find her own way to independence through a life of unremitting scholarship, editing, brief and meagerly supported field trips, and teaching.

So her personal life at this time was necessarily austere. For five days a week she had a room near Columbia, which she rented from a schoolteacher who used the apartment only over weekends, an economical but restrictive arrangement. There she did not have a single possession, not even a picture, of her own. Over weekends she would return to the charming small house in Bedford Hills to be with Stanley, with whom, however, communication was becoming more difficult with each passing year.

She took her degree after three semesters of study under Franz Boas and then, in the autumn of 1922, began teaching as his assistant at Barnard College. It was then, while I was an undergraduate, that I met her. For the following two years she continued to attend Boas' lectures.

Her first scholarly work in anthropology was carried out within the framework of historical diffusionist theory as taught by Boas. Both in her first publication, "The Vision in Plains Culture" (1922), and in her dissertation, "The Concept of the Guardian Spirit in North America" (1923a), she faithfully recorded and analyzed the extraordinary diversity of elements, each with a separate distribution, that became integrated in one culture in one way and in another culture quite differently.

In his teaching Boas rigorously criticized the theories of the nineteenth-century unilinear evolutionists, who held that all societies developed through an identical succession of stages. With equal vehemence he criticized the various theories of the extreme diffusionists—both the members of the English school (G. Elliot Smith, W. J. Perry, and their followers), who postulated a single origin for the world's cultures, and the members of the German school (Fritz Graebner, W. Koppers, W. Schmidt, and others), who attempted to trace the diffusion of culture traits and complexes (*Kulturkreise*) from a small number of ancient

WHEN
HER BEAUTY
WAS IN ECLIPSE,
AROUND 1924.

originating cultures. Boas himself had no use for any single, deterministic theory of the origins, forms, or development of the world's cultures.

Instead, in the training of his students Boas stressed the comparative method in which each trait or theme was traced in the most careful detail from one specific culture to another and, in each case, was placed within the context of the particular culture. Out of the discussions of problems that came up in seminars, students chose themes for further investigation. My own thesis, *An Inquiry into the Question of Cultural Stability in Polynesia* (1928), was an examination of a series of complexes—canoe-building, house-building, and tattooing—within a single culture area. Melville Herskovits, who was Ruth Benedict's contemporary, wrote his thesis on the cattle complex in East Africa (Herskovits, 1926). These were among the last dissertations prepared under Boas in which a student was asked to document the relationship between diffused elements and the life-style of a specific culture.

Years later Ruth Benedict asked Boas when he had given up his concentration on the problem of diffusion. He replied that it was in 1925, when he agreed to my going to Samoa. But, in fact, a year earlier he had set Ruth Bunzel to work on the problem of the individual's contribution to an art style, the outcome of which was her highly original book, *The Pueblo Potter: A Study of Creative Imagination in Primitive Art* (1929). From this time on, the scientific interests of Boas and many of his younger students moved in new directions.

Ruth Benedict, however, had begun her scholarly research before these interests emerged. It was her use of the theoretical premises of historical diffusionism in her first publications that later led A. R. Radcliffe-Brown to accuse her of having a "rags and tatters" approach to culture. As in the case of so many wittily destructive canards, Radcliffe-Brown's criticism has been frequently quoted and misquoted. In reality her presentation, as she developed it in these papers, indicates that she had already glimpsed what was to be her own great theoretical contribution to our understanding of the integration of each historically differentiated culture.

A more immediate appreciation of how she handled the problem in "The Concept of the Guardian Spirit in North America" came from Edward Sapir, who wrote her from Ottawa:

Dear Mrs. Benedict,

I read your paper yesterday in one breath, interrupted by supper, most necessary of distractions, only. Let me congratulate you on having produced a very fine piece of research. It makes a notable addition to the body of historical critiques that anthropology owes to Boas. I put it with such papers as Goldenweiser's "Totemism" [1910] and Waterman's "Exploratory Element in American Mythology" [1914] except that it impresses me as being decidedly more inspiring than either of these. A logical sequel (but one never works logically) is another paper on the historical development of the guardian spirit in a particular area, the idea being to show how the particular elements crystallized into the characteristic pattern. This "how" would involve consideration of some of the more general behavior patterns of the area or tribe and should perhaps show, unless you balk at psychology under all circumstances, how the crystallization could form a suitable frame for adequate individual expression. There is room somewhere for psychology—not so much as cultural determinant as incidental, but important, cultural content (or, better, utilization). Or do you take the extreme view (perhaps justifiable enough) that no matter what patterns rise, no matter how unsuitable they seem a priori for the guidance of human behavior, human psychology can and does accommodate itself to them as it accommodates itself to practically any physical environment? Culture then becomes merely environment for the individual psyche and can be made as much or as little of as this psyche pleases (or is allowed by its nature). And, conversely, culture, being historically moulded "environment" for individual living, can take no account whatever of the facts and theories of psychology. If you take this view, you need never discuss psychology as student of culture, but how then can you "evangelize" either? You would have to be a kind of culture fatalist. I should like to see the problem of individual and group psychology boldly handled, not ignored, by some one who fully understands culture as a historical entity. I hope you will do just this one of these days in connection with a concrete problem, whether guardian spirit or something else. (AAW: 49–50)

Her friendship with Sapir, which he initiated out of interest in her work as an anthropologist, developed rapidly and for the next three years was an important facet of her life. He was isolated and lonely in his post in Ottawa. He was working hard at linguistic texts but he was also writing and publishing verse. Ruth Benedict, caught between the demands of her professional commitment and those of her marriage, also was much alone. They soon discovered each other as poets; and poetry, and their own aspirations as poets, were the main bonds between them. In their voluminous correspondence (of which only Sapir's letters survive) they exchanged new poems, criticized each other's work, and discussed publication.

Ruth Benedict had published a number of poems before she came into anthropology. But now through her friendship with Sapir, as well as with Léonie Adams, Eda Lou Walton, and Louise Bogan, whom she met through me, she found herself for the first time among friends with whom she could discuss her poems, which she was still publishing under the pseudonym of Anne Singleton.

Although she had found in anthropology a discipline she respected and for which she was prepared to work very hard, poetry was still her most valued mode of expression. She did not yet think of anthropology as the field in which she could find full expression as the writer she hoped to become. She made a few experiments in writing descriptively about her field work, but essentially the two focuses of her interests did not merge. "Myth" (1949c) is one of the few poems in which she drew directly on anthropological sources for her imagery:

A god with tall crow feathers in his hair,
Long-limbed and bronzed, from going down of sun,
Dances all night upon his dancing floor,
Tight at his breast, our sorrows, one by one.

Relinquished stalks we could not keep till bloom,
And thorns unblossomed but of our own blood,
He gathers where we dropped them, filling full
His arms' wide circuit, briars and sterile shrub.

And all alone he dances, hour on hour,
Till all our dreams have blooming, and our sleep
Is odorous of gardens,—passing sweet
Beyond all, wearily, we till and reap.

In 1928, Ruth Benedict and Sapir both had completed manuscripts of verse, a good deal of which had already appeared in the little poetry magazines, among others *Poetry, The Measure, Palms,* and *Voices.* In the course of the year both offered their manuscripts to Louis Untermeyer at Harcourt Brace. Both were turned down.

Sapir had gone from Ottawa to the University of Chicago in 1925. There he became actively involved in administration, in setting up the Laboratory of Anthropology in Santa Fe, New Mexico, and in working on committees of the National Research Council. As his professional responsibilities expanded, he gradually turned away from poetry as a resource and a preoccupation. The attempt to publish the volume of collected verse was his last important effort to gain recognition as a poet. For Ruth Benedict also, the rejection of her manuscript of verse was decisive. Convinced by this that she was not justified in giving more time to writing poetry, she now devoted herself with greater assurance to anthropology.

Throughout the earlier years she held various nominal posts, first as assistant to Boas at Barnard and then, from 1923 on, as lecturer in anthropology at Columbia in a series of one-year appointments. In 1926–1927, she substituted for Gladys Reichard at Barnard; I was her assistant that year. Finally, in 1931, after she and Stanley Benedict separated, Boas obtained for her an appointment as assistant professor in the Department at Columbia, a post she held until 1937.

These appointments give little indication of the responsibilities she was taking on or of the role she was coming to play. Within the Department there were the graduate students who sought her out in the old seminar room on the seventh floor of the Journalism building where she worked during these early years. There were also the people in other disciplines who came to her for consultation and advice. In particular she developed a cooperative relationship with Wendall T. Bush in the Department of Religion at Columbia University and with Morris R. Cohen in the Department of Philosophy at City College, who had lectured in the Law School at Columbia in the summer of 1927. Within anthropology, as well, she was forming warm professional friendships. Then, in 1926, when she attended the International Congress of Americanists in Rome, and in 1928, when the Congress met in New York, she came to know a great many anthropologists from other parts of the world.

In the winter of 1925–1926, there was a new group of students in the Department. Among them were Melville Jacobs, Alexander Lesser, Thelma Adamson, Gene Weltfish, and Otto Klineberg, the psychologist who worked closely with Franz Boas on studies of race and the interpretation of facial expression. P. E. Goddard, at the American Museum of Natural History, nicknamed them "Jacob's gang," and initially Ruth did not find them very sympathetic. They clustered around Paul Radin—as students in my day had clustered around Alexander Goldenweiser—and asked him to give them, outside the Department, an informal "course."

Ruth Benedict's own fullest comments on the years between 1925 and 1933 are contained in the letters she wrote me while I was away on field trips in Samoa, in Manus, and in the Sepik area of New Guinea.

In March 1926 she wrote me about an unexpected visit to New York by Bronislaw Malinowski and about his encounter with Paul Radin and his circle of Columbia students. In the same letter she discussed the dif-

Arthur Muray

HER BEAUTY RESTORED, 1931.

ficulties of the Department seminar with the same uneasy complex of students:

I had such a good time yesterday with Malinowski. He turned up at lunch—no one knew he was here and asked to spend the afternoon with me. Radin came down for dinner, and afterwards he went to Radin's "course" and as soon as Radin threw the discussion open, Malinowski held forth. You'd like him a lot. He has the quick imagination and the by-play of mind that makes him a seven-days' joy, and he's discovered as if it were a new religion that acculturation makes so much difference that it hardly matters whether or not the trait is invented on the spot or diffused from some outside source. Of course it's just a swing of the pendulum to right the fantastic extremes of Eliott Smith and Graebner, but it's intriguing to find an intelligent person discovering with such force the things we've been brought up on with our mother's— or Papa Franz's!—milk. Give him time, and he'll discover with the same force that the little detail of independent invention or diffusion does make a difference in the picture after all. He starts of course from the premise that there's really no such phenomenon as an "invention"; it's all a very slow accretion that hardly, in its slow accumulation, gives more evidence of human inventiveness than borrowing does. He's right of course; it's just that he ought to say that for the purposes of his argument he's laying aside the problem of historical reconstruction from the distribution of traits, and of the differences between internal growth and stimulation from the outside—but why expect anyone who's just got religion to specify the things he's overlooked?

About psychoanalysis he's as skeptical as Papa Franz—nearly. He feels that no one now flies that banner except the extremists. The worth of it has been taken up into general psychological positions. Of course that's easy to say and overlooks the fact that they've been right before when they were outlawed and may be again. But anyway the orthodox will have nothing whatever to do with his work, of course. He and Papa Franz could agree to their hearts' content. Radin fumed all the evening. He's lectured me all the year about getting the good out of Eliott Smith et al. and of course about the great god Jung. It was fun to have so excellent an ally. Besides Radin hated my expositions of Boas. Malin-

27

owski liked to hear though and it was all to the good. He said, "if only I'd known, Boas was my spiritual father all the time," and "You must tell me what Boas has been teaching for twenty years about this and that, or I'll be discovering it as if it had never happened to anybody before."

At the evening session he rather pointedly ignored Radin—whom he very obviously has a fondness for—and we all had a good time. You'd have thought we were all ardent diffusionists, and I'd been expecting to see the whole set run down Boas and his mechanical interpretations. There's rather a lot of the feeling abroad, I think, but I see the younger set, "Jacob's gang" very casually and never to talk anthropology.

The seminar [at Columbia] is going to be just as difficult as I thought. We had stupid discussions on the diffusionists' positions, and that included Dr. Boas's work; the point I made was that studies of distribution really had it as their objective to put the problem before us, not to solve any of them. Dr. Boas in some moods would say that himself, but it troubled him just the same. Then this week Klineberg—do you remember the very fair, neat-minded boy in psychology—reported on psychoanalytic treatment of myth. I told him to do it as sympathetically as possible, and he thought at first that with the best will in the world that was impossible. But with the help of Malinowski's work and of suggestions we cooked up, he gave an exceedingly interesting report. I think Boas would accept all of it but the terminology—but that kills it. He won't talk about a repression. He'll say that people have a drive to make fun of their taboos, but to call it compensation for an inhibition—that is beyond the pale. He got very excited and it made a very good discussion; we haven't talked about it since but Goddard says he was really stirred up. It's curious. (AAW: 304–6)

With the exception of her first brief summer field trip in 1922 to the Serrano, whose old culture was fragmented beyond the possibility of adequate reconstruction, all of Ruth Benedict's early work was with library materials. She found fascinating the whole intricate process of piecing together bits, filling in lacunae, and discovering correspondences and congruences in the scattered and uneven accounts of vanished and of almost extinct cultures. It was an engrossing puzzle and all her life she enjoyed the complexities of fashioning an image of a culture out of imperfect materials even more than she did her own field work or reading the finished work of those anthropologists who were working on living cultures.

This willingness to do painstaking, exacting, detailed research made more or less inevitable the kinds of tasks that Boas found for her to do. At a time when sources of money for research were extremely limited, Boas had to stretch his very meager funds as far as possible to help those who most needed help. Obviously, as the wife of a professor at Cornell Medical College, Ruth Benedict was not in actual need. The fact that she was struggling for independence did not change this in Boas' view. What he found for her was an occupation, supported by small grants from the Southwest Society—the medium through which Elsie Clews Parsons poured money into Boas' enterprises. The task Ruth Benedict undertook was making folklore concordances and editing the *Journal of American Folklore*, of which she was the editor from 1925 to 1939.

In the 1920s, in spite of the growing number of graduate students—women as well as men—who were working under Boas, the Department was very weak. Boas himself had tenure, but the university administration, which had never forgiven him for taking a neutralist stand in World War I, gave him only the most minimal assistance. Boas himself was very exceptional in the number of graduate women students he accepted, and no other anthropology department in the country had such a large proportion of women among those to whom degrees were awarded.[3] But the idea that a woman might become a member of the faculty did not then occur to the administration. However, when Ruth Benedict finally separated from Stanley, she asked Boas for some firmer position. Now, recognizing her need as well as the responsible role she filled in the Department, he went to work and in 1931 obtained the assistant professorship for her—but without tenure.

During these years she began to go on summer field trips. In the summer of 1924 she made her first field trip to Zuni. In 1925 she worked in Zuni and Cochiti. In 1927 she worked among the Pima. In 1931, under

[3] In the years between 1901 and 1940, during which 51 doctoral degrees in anthropology were awarded at Columbia University, 29 were awarded to men and 22 to women, beginning with Laura L. Benedict in 1914 (Thomas, 1955: 703–8).

the auspices of the Southwest Laboratory of Anthropology, she supervised a student field trip to the Mescalero Apache, in which Fred Eggan, Jules Henry, Morris Opler, and Sol Tax participated as students. Eight years later, in 1939, she supervised an anthropological field workshop among the Blackfoot in Montana and Alberta, Canada. Among those who participated were Jane Richardson and Lucien M. Hanks, Gitel Posnansky and Robert Steed, Oscar and Ruth Lewis, and Esther Goldfrank, who joined the group as a senior colleague (Goldfrank, 1945). In contrast to the Apache field trip, where the whole group worked closely together, the participants this time were dispersed among the Blood, the Northern and Southern Piegan, and the Northern Blackfoot (Skisika), a far less valuable experience for a group of young fieldworkers. After a short stay in Montana, Ruth Benedict herself joined the group working with the Blood.[4]

Although she respected field work and emphasized the great importance of the field methods taught by Boas, including meticulous, verbatim recording of informants' words, field work for her was always arduous. Her deafness made learning a language or even taking linguistic texts impracticable. The bulk of her work was with individual informants who, hour after hour, dictated in English or through an interpreter the endless, repetitious pueblo folktales.

Living in the field was comfortless. There were always difficulties about obtaining food and she was harassed by bedbugs. And even though the pueblos retained a great deal of their old culture, change was going on and she was under constant strain listening for the older culture beneath the broken phrases of the new.

Nevertheless she did enough field work to understand very well many of the problems of modern field research. She was once summoned before the ceremonial leaders in Zuni and commanded by them to explain her presence. She worked in Zuni when it was no longer possible to photograph there, after an episode in which a young psychologist was stoned and had his camera broken (Pandey, 1972), and fieldworkers were barely tolerated. Originally she had been told that she might have to persuade an informant to leave the pueblo and work with her in a distant place. Her request for assistance in this evoked an outburst in a letter to

---

[4] Personal communication, Esther Goldfrank Wittvogel.

her from Jaime de Angulo, the California linguist, that is curiously re-
miniscent of many of today's protests against the work of professional anthropologists:

>   *As for helping you to get an informant, and the way you de-*
> *scribe it "if I took him with me to a safely American place" . . . "an*
> *informant who would be willing to give tales and ceremonials" . . . oh*
> *God! Ruth, you have no idea how much that has hurt me. I don't know*
> *how I am going to be able to talk to you about it because I have a sin-*
> *cere affection for you. But do you realize that it is just that sort of thing*
> *that kills the Indians? I mean it seriously. It kills them spiritually first,*
> *and as in their life the spiritual and the physical element are much more*
> *interdependent than in our own stage of culture, they soon die of it*
> *physically. They just lie down and die. That's what you anthropologists*
> *with your infernal curiosity and your thirst for scientific data bring*
> *about.*
>
>   *Don't you understand the psychological value of secrecy at a certain*
> *level of culture? Surely you must, but you have probably never con-*
> *nected it with this. You know enough of analytical psychology to know*
> *that there are things that must not be brought to the light of day,*
> *otherwise they wither and die like uprooted plants.*
>
>   *Have you never lived with Indians, Ruth? I really don't know, that's*
> *why I ask you. Is your own interest in primitive religion the result of a*
> *deep but unacknowledged mysticism? . . .*
>
>   *Why do you want to know these things? Of course if you promised*
> *that you would never publish the actual secrets, I would help you all I*
> *can. I would tell you a lot myself about the meaning of the whole thing.*
> *It is all right to talk about it in a general way, with certain reserva-*
> *tions, the necessary care that must be always used in handling all eso-*
> *teric knowledge. It is as powerful and dangerous as the lightning. Look*
> *at all the harm that raw psychoanalysts do to their patients. . . . But*
> *the actual details of ceremonies, that must never be told. They are as*
> *much part and parcel of the mind of the believer as the pyramidal cells*
> *of his cortex. They belong to him. They belong to the secret society. They*
> *have a real, actual meaning and value, as secrets, for the members of*
> *the society. You must not rob them. You must not sneak into their*

house. You wouldn't inveigle my child into telling you the secrets of my home. (AAW: 296–97)

She herself had no doubt that recording the fast-vanishing knowledge of myths and ceremonies was a valuable thing to do both for the sake of the Indians themselves and for the great contribution the recorded materials made to man's storehouse of information about diverse cultures.

In spite of the handicaps under which she worked and the uncertainties of field work in the pueblos, her responses to the field situation were vivid and visually acute and her relations with her informants were lively and realistically appreciative. In the summer of 1925, while I was on my way to Samoa, she wrote me long letters from Zuni and later from Cochiti.

In a letter of August 15, she described one of her Zuni informants:

Nick and Flora both eat out of my hand this summer. Nick is invaluable—if I could only take his "singsongs" in text! The stories he tells which he calls "sacred stories" are as endless in ceremonial details as Flora's, so I guess the general type is established beyond question as far as Zuñi goes. I shall end by being fond of Nick. He told me the emergence story with fire in his eye yesterday through twenty-two repetitions of the same episode in twenty-two "sacred" songs. He'd try to skip but habit was too strong. He would only interrupt, "Zame zing, zame zing"—and go on with the same endless phrases to the end. There's something impressive in the man's fire. He might have been a really great man. And yet I think any society would have used its own terms to brand him as a witch. He's too solitary and too contemptuous. . . . (AAW: 292)

And on August 24, her last day in Zuni, she wrote:

Ruth Bunzel came by Friday's mail wagon. Yesterday we went up under the sacred mesa along stunning trails where the great wall towers above you always in new magnificence. . . . When I'm God I'm going to build my city there. (AAW: 293)

After a brief stay in Peña Blanca, where she waited in vain for the arrival of an adequate informant, she went on to Cochiti, where she wrote me on September 3:

The cart came, and we lunged across the river and up to this quite charming pueblo. I'm glad I spent so much time with my mountains in Peña Blanca, for here, being so near them, we can't see them at all. My house is next door to a half-underground kiva with its ladder thrust up to the sky. An adobe stairway ascends from one side. It's quite effective. The houses many of them have twisted acacias to sit under in front, and porches covered with boughs whose leaves have turned just the color of the adobe. In Zuñi you would never sit out unless it was about to rain because no shade is thought proper in Zuñi.

There are drawbacks in this abode. The menu is somewhat difficult since neither bread nor milk are known here. I've decided on rice and raisins as my staple, and there are some canned soups in the store. Presently the Indians will begin to provide, and I'll be eating field corn with the rest of them. —The worst is as usual, and I haven't had time to get them tamed down at all. I'm renting the house from an old Indian who was an old, old-time graduate of Carlisle and who speaks English with notable precision. He said farewell the first night, and then: "Well, friend, you'll be troubled by bugs some. There were none here, but our neighbors kept chickens in the back yard. We came in a week or two ago—(they're out "on the farm" now)—and it was awful. At that time we saw them crawling in lines in the cracks of the floor." Therefore as soon as he'd left I managed to scramble up an amputated ladder to the roof with my bedding on my back. It was much better, but even daytime gives no surcease as yet.

I don't understand the openness with which they give me the stories. They don't seem in the least secretive before the rest. Dr. Boas thought I ought not to set foot myself in Cochiti if I were going to be within a hundred miles with an informant. But there is no trace of the Zuñi intensity of feeling. Of course I am getting very unesoteric stories, but if I sit long enough, I don't doubt getting the other kind. I never do get this sense of the spiked dangerous fence that Elsie [Clews Parsons], and Dr. Boas in this case, make so much of. (AAW: 298–99)

On September 5, she continued her description of work in Cochiti:

I have male callers, mother callers, innumerable children who've heard I have candy, and the family of the house wander in at least every day from the farm across the river. There'll be a dance tomorrow, too;—I don't expect much. "Young Horse Dance" they call it. I see they've set up four posts in the Plaza that are probably the hitching posts!

My diet is expanding. The chief difficulty was that I was wholly unprepared to find flour unknown in these stores. But the keeper of one of these little rows of shelves they call "stores"—there are two— unearthed three little cartons of Aunt Jemima pancake flour, and I am saved. . . .

My old man is ninety and a great old charater. He must have been fair as a white girl in his day—he's known all over his country as "the Fair" (blonde). He speaks excellent Spanish and I can follow a good deal when he talks it—I am angry that I have to bother with interpreters at all, but I do. He hobbles along on his cane, bent nearly double, and is still easily the most vivid personage in the landscape—he has the habit of enthusiasm and of good fellowship. (AAW: 300)

She made the most of her own field work, but I think she got greater enjoyment out of working over her students' field notes, teaching them how to organize them and trying to make a whole out of their often scattered observations. She was openly impatient with my growing emphasis on the need to prepare students for the physical difficulties of field work and for the problems of relations with officials and settlers and traders whom they might encounter in the field. Like Franz Boas, she felt that students who had been exposed to enough field material—ethnographic, textual, and linguistic—would be able to go out and fend for themselves.

In September 1926, Ruth Benedict and I attended the International Congress of Americanists in Rome. That summer, while she was traveling alone in Europe, she had her hair cut. It had turned white prematurely and she was once more extraordinarily beautiful. At this time I was on my way home from Samoa. I brought with me a host of new problems, psychological problems for the most part that were related to Reo Fortune's psychological interests. On the ship coming home Ruth and I began a discussion that continued for many years.

It was my view that an approach to an understanding of the way in which culture determines psychological behavior—the phrase "culture and personality" was not yet in use—would involve the establishment of systematic relationships between universal characteristics of the human mind and the ways in which these universals, which someday would be charted and described, were represented in specific cultures.

Ruth Benedict, however, contended that any theory of the relationship of culture to dreams, for example, provides only one way of looking at the materials and that there are innumerable other ways of doing so, no one of them necessarily more "correct" than another. She saw any partic- ular way of organizing data, such as the attempt made by W. H. R. Rivers to relate neurophysiology and dreams (Rivers, 1923), as providing one version of reality—a version, in Rivers' case, that was expressive of his temperament and experience but that contained no absolute truth on which it was possible to build a system.

On her next summer's field trip to the Pima (1927) she first recognized the tremendous contrasts between the cultures of the pueblos and the cul- tures of the Plains. Needing terms of reference she adopted, as metaphor- ic descriptions of these contrasts, Nietzsche's categories of Apollonian and Dionysian. Out of this sudden awareness she began to develop her own configurational approach to culture.

During the following winter (1927–1928) our discussions continued while Ruth Benedict worked on her paper, "Psychological Types in the Cultures of the Southwest" (1930d), in which she first worked out this configurational approach, and I wrote my monograph on Samoa, *Social Organization of Manu'a* (1930). In the course of this I attempted a brief delineation of "dominant cultural attitudes," as an application of the con- figurational approach to a living, ongoing culture.

At the same time Ruth Benedict was working on an essay on religion for the textbook, *General Anthropology* (Boas, 1938), that Boas had fi- nally decided it would be desirable to publish. He had always disapproved of textbooks as it was his view that by the time a principle of social behav- ior became well established it was a truism. However, textbooks had come into wide use—including those by Robert Lowie (1920), Alexander Goldenweiser (1922), Alfred Kroeber (1923), and Clark Wissler (1929). Consequently, Boas felt it was worthwhile to bring together materials representative of his viewpoint. Religion was a subject on which Ruth Benedict had lectured and on which she was considering writing a book. In the chapter on religion written for *General Anthropology* (Benedict, 1938b), as in her earlier article on magic, prepared for the *Encyclopedia of the Social Sciences* (Benedict, 1933a), she based the distinction she made between religion and magic primarily on differences in the attitudes of the suppliant and the practitioner. Thereafter, except when it was necessary for some formal reason, she never again wrote about religion.[5]

The International Congress of Americanists, at which she presented her paper on "Psychological Types in the Cultures of the Southwest," met in New York in September 1928. As I had already left for the field again, she wrote me a long letter describing the meetings:

> *There've been no casualties. Papa Franz has even had a good time since the first day, and nothing has gone conspicuously wrong. [Waldemar] Bogoras retails how at the Congress in 1902 they shook the hand of the President of the United States in Washington and were taken out to the desert of the Southwest and given shovels to dig up whatever they should find; it was all "planted" and there was a speech about all that they were being given under the "fresh dust of centuries"—so he says this is a one-horse funeral. But he's otherwise placid, and there seems to be no general demand for the unattainable, like planted potsherds, and Calvin Coolidge's hand. . . .*
>
> *I must begin farther back. The formal opening was notable for the fact that, just as Papa Franz had planned, [Henry Fairfield] Osborn played second fiddle. That morning a note had come down from Osborn's office saying that the President must make the first and opening address. Up goes Papa Franz and beards the lion in his den, and when they are seated on the platform, sure enough it's Papa Franz that gets up. . . . There was a very excellent tribute to Papa Franz from dear*

---

[5] Shortly before she died, she had agreed to prepare a chapter on religion for *Dynamic Psychiatry*, the volume edited by Franz Alexander and Helen Ross (1952), but it was never written.

old Professor [Albrecht] Penck who is a great beaming child loving all the world and who holds his hand pressed tight against his bow window as if he were feeling for his heart beat; he spoke of the greatest of anthropologists of German birth, Professor Boas, "for we of my country have sent to you our best." It was very good. . . .

I've had good talks with Bogoras. He's full of the "new dawn" and sure as a child. From now on man no longer fears circumstance, he is released, a new man. Of course this has put an end to our enjoyment of some of the old classics of literature; even Dostoievsky is a little dated, and Tolstoi and Turgenev are out of the running. But Tchekov is untouched—and who else do you think? I'd give you one hundred guesses. It's Anatole France. I was completely aghast. I instanced the Red Lily and he granted that the Red Lily wasn't a good book to illustrate his side of the point. He says that's general intellectuals' opinion in Soviet Russia. Then there's [William] Thalbitzer who looks old and scarred. He's like a patient academic Christus, and likes to talk to me. . . .

I might get around to the papers too. [Wilhelm] Koppers is here to talk for [Fritz] Graebner; the only thing I can think of when he talks is that I'd like to go to confession to him. He [is] sure of himself, and probably abominably dogmatic, but he has that authority that we don't know how to come by in this country. Kroeber always gets up after Koppers or [Max] Uhle or a paper by [Louis] Capitan and says a little speech about how we all agree; then up hops Papa Franz and says "But it seems to my mind that there is a fundamental difference," which he proceeds to expound. There was a lot of interest in my paper and it had an excellent place on the program, just before the luncheon at the Heye Museum. Kroeber's question was just, "How does the old man take a paper like that?" Edward[Sapir] said it was a good lecture and a good point, and [Alfred] Kidder came up to say it was illustrated just as much by the pueblo art and material culture as by their religion. Wissler scowled through a great deal of it and I haven't seen him since; Elsie [Clews Parsons] was speechless and rose to make all sorts of pointless addenda when she recovered her breath. Professor [Theodor-Wilhelm] Danzel—the one from Hamburg, who's been staying with Gladys [Reichard]—said it was the most important paper of the Congress and agreed with work of his own; the same from [Hortense]

37

Powdermaker. I had to do it all in less than twenty minutes so it had to be too schematic, but for the given length of time I think it was as good as I could have made it. . . . (AAW: 306–8)

PATTERNS OF CULTURE

In the spring of 1932, while Alfred Kroeber was visiting professor in the Department, Ruth Benedict finally decided to write a book based on the idea of cultural configurations. There was a certain irony in this decision.

Early in 1931 Boas offered Kroeber the chairmanship of the Department as his chosen successor (T. Kroeber, 1970: 155). The offer grew out of the long and close professional association and warm friendship between the older and the younger man. Kroeber was attracted by the opportunity to return to New York, where he had been born and still had many ties, but in the end he chose to remain with the department he had built up at the University of California in Berkeley. To please Boas, however, he agreed to come to Columbia for one semester in 1932.

At this time Kroeber had already begun to develop his own elaborate and beautiful treatment of cultural configurations with its emphasis on aesthetic and intellectual achievement in a historical framework. At Columbia he planned to give lectures on world civilization, a theme that was congruent with his current preoccupations. Instead, Boas, in his characteristic peremptory way, insisted that Kroeber give a course on the cultures of Highland South America, a subject from which he had, at the time, moved away. Kroeber acquiesced reluctantly. But Ruth Benedict felt that both his lectures and his contributions to seminars were very dry. It was her exasperation at this—for she had a sense of the genuine compatibility between Kroeber's approach to culture and her own—that drove her to make the impulsive decision to write her own book.

This was the book that became *Patterns of Culture.* She worked on the manuscript on and off for the next two years. During most of that period I was in the field, in New Guinea, and her letters to me, as well as several exchanges of letters with Reo Fortune about the use of his Dobuan material (Fortune, 1932), provide the best record of her ups and downs in thinking through the problems of the book.

She was explicit in her initial decision to use material that she could trust because she knew it well and had discussed it with the fieldworker himself. For Zuni she could draw on her own and Ruth Bunzel's field materials. Everyone who did research in Zuni worked with the same informants, so that even I, who had never been in Zuni, could distinguish between the dreams of Flora and Margaret in Ruth Bunzel's dream collection. Ruth Benedict also knew the literature on Zuni inside out and she had done intensive background work on Zuni versions of widespread myths, one of the most readily documented aspects of work on a vanishing culture, which she later published in *Zuni Mythology* (1935a).

For the Northwest Coast, the second culture she discussed, she had full access to Boas' materials, published and unpublished, and she spent many hours of discussion with him over the handling of details.

Eventually she decided that she needed a third culture, and in August 1932 she wrote to me:

I wrote a letter to Reo last week when I was turning over in my mind the choice of illustrative chapters in my book. I've written him an outline of the book, so stop and read it. If I were properly forethoughtful I'd have thought the problem all out six months ago and had his answer by this time. But I hadn't really thought I'd need to take one of yours or Reo's cultures—because you do them so well I can only parrot your points. And with the pueblos and the [Northwest Coast] that isn't so. But there just isn't any assurance in using other people's cultures for a discussion like this (other field workers', I mean). Even in North America I can't do anything but guess. And in Africa it's hopeless. . . .

I've turned over titles and titles. I want the title of the book to clearly indicate that my competence is in anthropology, nothing else. That is, I don't want any psychologizing title. I shall suggest "Primitive Peoples: An Introduction to Cultural Types." Have you suggestions? It can be changed much later.

I hadn't realized till I came to plan this work how all the points I've worked on all fall into the same outline. (AAW: 321–22)

Early in October she again wrote to me about the manuscript:

> *The first four chapters of my book are ready, and I am holding them till the next boat thinking I can get two more to put with them. It's hard with classes beginning and reviewing and the rest but you'd be amazed at the work I get done. Or I hope you would. It's an improvement anyway. It makes me realize how much energy always went into the mere background of living at all. . . . I don't write verses anymore, but in my present mood I can well do without them. . . . Your comment on my liking bad scrappy ethnology better than good and finished work (La Flesche died last month) came just in time to amuse me while I was doing Kwakiutl. For of course I enjoyed it. Tons of raw material entirely reliable, and a minimum of interpretation or explanation. Of course it's not true that I like it better than Dobu [Fortune, 1932], for instance, or Manus Social Organization [Mead, 1930], but it's a kind of field work where I don't have to go around to feasts or lay myself out to stupid old women, and of course I enjoy it. (AAW: 323–24)*

A week later she wrote:

> *I'm so glad you came to the same conclusion I had about the material I could use for the configuration point. In ["Configurations of Culture in North America"] I didn't have any sense of attempting to prove the Navaho Dionysian, but only of showing where their reported burial customs tied up in the general distribution of traits. But of course I can't use them, or even Plains, for a description of the way their culture worked. (AAW: 324)*

It is very important, I think, to document how she came to use the Dobuan material in *Patterns of Culture*—that she chose this culture not because it complemented in any systematic fashion the other two cultures she had chosen but because she knew and trusted the fieldworker who had done the research. In the letter she wrote Reo Fortune in August 1932 giving her reasons for wanting to use Dobuan culture as her third example, she also described her intentions in general:

The theme of course is cultural configurations again. There's a first chapter on Anthropology Old and New, which is all old stuff about giving up the concept of THE primitive, etc. It says many of the same things I said in that old Century article ["The Science of Custom"] about the point of anthropology. Then there's a chapter on the Diversity of Culture, how cultures become so different according to the different aspects of life they capitalize, and how the interpenetration of traits makes for still more diversity. The next chapter is the Integration of Culture, which is a chapter giving the reasons for thinking that cultures should be studied as configurations, and speaking of the Germans who've tried. Then there's a long discussion of the pueblos, contrasting them too with the rest of North America. That's the next chapter, and long. I'll make there the same points at more length that are in ["Configurations of Culture in North America"] and ["Anthropology and the Abnormal"]. For the third example I'd choose to use Dobu. The only thing against it is that you've already put it in shape and said the things that need saying. It isn't as it is with the Southwest and the Northwest Coast, a reworking of raw materials. But Dobu is so good, and I feel so strongly that I wouldn't venture to use a culture that I knew wholly out of a book without having the chance to talk about it to the person who knows it—that I've decided to go ahead and write the chapter. I can make it a discussion that will mostly call attention to your "sensational material," and direct people to it. And people need to be told in words of two syllables what contrasting cultures mean. I wish I knew how you reacted to it. You have said it so well in your book that I can only sponge. On the other hand I could use Dobu better than any other as a background for the last chapter—or I think there'll be two—of the book, which will be an expansion of the Culture and the Abnormal paper, a discussion of the adjustment of the individual to his cultural type.

If you think it would be awful of me to take the words out of your mouth this way, cable me collect, just "Don't," and I'll understand. But as this couldn't come till after the chapter was written you'll get a carbon of my draft anyway.[6] In the chapter on Integration I dicuss my

---

[6] In those days mail to New Guinea came by sea and, coming from New York, took a minimum of three months to reach us in the field.

> *reasons for choosing just these three cultures, and say that I've both been able to talk them over with the persons who've done the field work, and that the chapters have been read by the field workers. So I'll get the Dobu chapter off to you for blue pencilling just as soon as I can.* (AAW: 320–21)

Months later, writing from the Sepik River, Reo Fortune replied:

> *Of course use the Dobuan material if it's really good enough. I like it very well that you think it's such, and then like it very well again and then have no different feeling.* (AAW: 329)

Once the choice had been made, Ruth Benedict realized how she could weave the Dobuan material into her discussion of deviance. For readers this tended to obscure the grounds on which the original choice had been made. It reflects a familiar dilemma in anthropology. For any group of cultures, however chosen, will form a pattern—the more so when the writer had in mind a pattern—without violating the materials. This comes about because there are so many possible comparisons that can be made within any selected set of cultures.

As she had earlier used Nietzsche's terms, Apollonian and Dionysian, adapting them to her own purposes, now she borrowed from psychiatry the terms *paranoid* and *megalomaniac* in her characterizations of the Dobuan and Kwakiutl cultures without any deeper sense that the use of these terms implied a specific theoretical orientation on her part.

The idea that there are systematic relationships between universal psychological types was one that she had been discussing with me and with Sapir ever since I had attended the Toronto meetings of the British Association for the Advancement of Science in 1924, where there had been discussions of Jung's *Psychological Types* (1923), which had recently been published in English, and Seligman's article, also recently published, "Anthropology and Psychiatry: A Study of Some Points of Contact" (1923), in which he suggested that cultures might be thought of in psychiatric terms.

But Ruth Benedict was not considering cultures in this way. She was not dealing with any of the limitations imposed by some strict theory of epigenetic stages, or of critical periods in child development, or of a closed typological system based on a limited set of human potentialities, whether the types were somatotypic, endocrinologic, or derived from the analysis of cases around the world that had come to the attention of psychiatrists or psychoanalysts. She was dealing with an open system. Her intention was to present examples of the way cultures emphasize different aspects of personality, each one stressing some part of the wide arc of human potentialities.

She stated this quite clearly in our correspondence about the manuscript:

> *You write about the numbers of configuration classifications you might get by going through the cultures of the world, and how helpless we are without stable classifications the psychologists ought to have provided us with. It would make it neater if they had, but I don't know that it would be any guarantee of good anthropological work in cultures. I feel about it just as I do about a novelist's getting down his character with the correct motivations, etc.; it might help him to have had Freud investigate it for him first, but usually all it's done is to take his eyes off the real person he's describing, and it's actually vitiated more character-drawing than it's helped. I know I feel that way about it because what I'm fundamentally interested in is the character of the culture and the relation of that institutionalized character to the individual of that culture. I can see that there are other problems, but I can't see that we're in a position yet to deal with them.* (AAW: 324)

She wanted to demonstrate that culture can be seen as "personality writ large," that is, that each historical culture represents a many-generational process of paring, sifting, adapting, and elaborating on an available areal form, and that each culture, in turn, shapes the choices of those born and living within it.

She recognized that there are individuals whose temperaments, given by heredity, are so alien to the emphases of their culture that they cannot adapt themselves to it easily if at all. This explanation made plausible her own lifelong sense of incompatibility with the culture in which she lived. But here again the position she took was based not on current psychological theories but on ethnographic observations of particular—and contrasting—cultural styles. Where she was clearly ahead of her time was in her recognition that, within any culture, the institutionalized forms of behavior available to the deviant or the unstable individual are culturally determined. In her article "Anthropology and the Abnormal" (1934a, p. 77) she wrote:

> *The baldest evidences of cultural patterning in the behavior of unstable individuals is in trance phenomena. The use to which such proclivities are put, the form their manifestations take, the things that are seen and felt in trance, are all culturally controlled. The tranced individual may come back with communications from the dead describing the minutiae of life in the hereafter, or he may visit the world of the unborn, or get information about lost objects in the camp, or experience cosmic unity, or acquire a life-long guardian spirit, or get information about coming events. Even in trance the individual holds strictly to the rules and expectations of his culture, and his experience is as locally patterned as a marriage rite or an economic exchange.*

Essentially, it was her use of psychiatric terms to describe cultures (even her use of the term *type*, which implied the existence of a typology as well as her use of terms such as *deviant*, which had been preempted by professional psychology) that was misleading and that resulted in a great many misunderstandings and misinterpretations of her theoretical position. Much of the criticism directed against *Patterns of Culture* was based on her critics' failure to grasp that she was not dealing with typologies in the sense that cultures can be seen as elaborating psychological or biological givens.

But the very absence of any such binding psychological or biological theory is what has allowed the book to survive all through the theoretical controversies of the last forty years. It is soundly based in careful ethnographic descriptions of well-observed cultures, and no part of the description is compromised by outmoded theory or questionable hypotheses. She wanted to demonstrate what an extraordinary range of cultures had existed and might exist—and she succeeded magnificently.

There were, however, other critics and other kinds of misunderstanding of her intentions. Melville Herskovits, in his book *Franz Boas: The Science of Man in the Making* (1953, p. 71) commented:

> *Broader uses of psychological concepts, such as those which attempted to assign entire societies to particular categories of mental set, as in the book* Patterns of Culture *by his student and colleague Ruth Benedict, seemed to him to raise methodological questions that had not been faced. Though for personal reasons he consented to write a brief preface for the work, he devoted several paragraphs to a critical discussion of the problem in his chapter on methods of research in the textbook he edited, especially pointed because he takes as his example the Northwest Coast Indians, who had been cited as an extreme case by Benedict. Indicating that "the leading motive of their life is the limitless pursuit of gaining social prestige and of holding on to what has been gained, and the intense feeling of inferiority and shame if even a part of the prestige is lost," he adds, "these tendencies are so striking that the amiable qualities that appear in intimate family life are easily overlooked." Certainly the almost paranoid nature of the behavior of this people as portrayed by Benedict is scarcely in line with the patterns of humility Boas sketches as prevailing within the family. He summarizes his own position with characteristic scientific realism and methodological caution: "The less pronounced the leading ideas of a simple culture, or the more varying the ideas of a tribe divided into social strata, the more difficult it is to draw a valid picture that does not contain contradictions. We cannot hope to do more than to elucidate the leading ideas, remembering clearly the limitations of their validity."*

Herskovits then began the next paragraph: "None of the approaches to human mentality that derive from the study of psychopathology ever appealed to Boas." By implication this was what Ruth Benedict had done.

In fact, Boas had followed every stage in the development of her theory, and his comment that "we cannot hope to do more than to elucidate the leading ideas, remembering clearly the limitations of their validity" (Boas, 1938, p. 685) is as definite an affirmation of her theoretical position as is his statement in the Introduction to *Patterns of Culture* (p. xiii):

> As the author points out, not every culture is characterized by a dominant character, but it seems probable that the more intimate our knowledge of the cultural drives that actuate the behaviour of the individual, the more we shall find that certain controls of emotion, certain ideals of conduct, prevail that account for what seem to us as abnormal attitudes when viewed from the standpoint of our civilization. The relativity of what is considered social or asocial, normal or abnormal, is seen in a new light.
>
> The extreme cases selected by the author make clear the importance of the problem.

The astonishing thing is that Herskovits entirely overlooked Ruth Benedict's own much earlier statement of the point in her paper, *Configurations of Culture in North America* (1930d, p. 22, fn. 37):

> It is obvious from the nature of the case that this Northwest Coast game of prestige can only be played by selected members of the community. A large proportion of the tribe is no more than audience to these principal players, and the configuration of life for them necessarily differs. We need particularly to understand these "fan" cultures and the psychological attitudes characteristic on the one hand of the actors and on the other of those who make up the audience.

Other critics misrepresented the sources of her ideas. For example, Victor Barnouw, who had been her student, wrote in a long obituary article (Barnouw, 1949, pp. 242-43):

> Willingly Anne Singleton slipped on the rough hair shirt of discipline, took upon herself the exacting Boas regimen of hard work, read endlessly, endured the discomforts of ethnological field work, and finally emerged as "Dr. Benedict." But it is a measure of her individuality that Ruth Benedict never became a mere rubber stamp of the old man's thinking. In fact, her work represents a marked contrast to his. Boas had long ago rejected the "deep" intuitive plunges of German scholarship and philosophy; but in these same dubious sources Ruth Benedict now found inspiration. Under her master's somewhat jaun-

diced eye she turned to Nietzsche, Spengler and Dilthey, whose ideas she somehow blended with the Boas tradition of intensive field work in a particular area. From this unexpected amalgam she managed to fashion her famous Patterns of Culture.

The facts, as Barnouw could have ascertained, were quite different.[7] Boas himself insisted that she discuss earlier German works that had a faint relationship to her thought. This was in keeping with his European scholarly insistence on establishing theoretical genealogies. So he introduced her to Dilthey, as Sapir had introduced her to Spengler. But neither writer had shaped her ideas.

Quite different criticisms were made of her picture of Zuni, in which she emphasized the ideal pattern of harmonious relations. The analysis of Ruth Bunzel's case studies, which she made available to Irving Goldman (1937) when we were doing the background research for *Cooperation and Competition among Primitive Peoples* (Mead, 1937), showed that personal life among the Zuni contrasted as markedly with the harmonies of their expressed cultural ideals as, among the Kwakiutl, in Boas' own description, the "amiable qualities" of family life contrasted with their "limitless pursuit of gaining social prestige and holding on to what has been gained" (Boas, 1938, p. 685). A still different viewpoint was expressed by a Chinese investigator (Li An-che, 1937), who found that much that Ruth Benedict had described as special in Zuni culture seemed to him quite natural and ordinary.

In preparing promotional material on *Patterns of Culture* the publishers added their own quota of misinterpretation. But the original jacket copy which she herself had prepared stated the central issue quite simply:

In a straightforward style, the author demonstrates how the manners and morals of these tribes, and our own as well, are not piecemeal items of behavior, but consistent ways of life. They are not racial, nor the necessary consequence of human nature, but have grown up historically in the life history of the community. (AAW: 212)

[7] For a much later, retrospective discussion of *Patterns of Culture* by the same critic, see Barnouw (1957).

In the early 1930s, when Ruth Benedict was working on *Patterns of Culture*, very little modern field work had as yet been done in living cultures. This meant that there was almost no basis on which significant comparisons could be made of the culturally distinct ways in which individuals, within a wide range of temperaments, slowly and inevitably, through a series of culturally regular childrearing experiences, attained a culturally regular character structure. For systematic research on this problem to be carried out it was necessary to have a dynamic theory of personality development. In time, the Freudian model in its various versions, a learning theory model (on which work was just then beginning at Yale), and a Gestalt psychology model would each provide links between the biologically given and cultural experience. But no such models were available to Ruth Benedict in her work with American Indian materials when she wrote *Patterns of Culture*. Boas' lectures on learning leaned heavily on theories of imitation and on the conception of "automatic behavior"—the phrase he used to describe the unexamined and unselfconscious performance of a culturally defined role.

Ruth Benedict's deepest interest was in the *products* of culture—in high cultures, in literature and poetry, and to some extent in architecture and painting. Her deafness and perhaps the lack of some innate dependence on sound patterns made music inaccessible to her. She saw primitive cultures as in themselves works of art to be preserved for the world. In this she shared the point of view that Kroeber expressed so well in the prologue/epilogue to his work on Mohave myths and literature:

> *I have long pondered to whom we owe the saving of human religious and aesthetic achievements such as are recorded here. It is probably not to the group that produced them. Why should we preserve Mohave values when they themselves cannot preserve them, and their descendants will likely be indifferent? It is the future of our own world culture that can be enriched by the preservation of these values, and our ultimate understandings grow wider as well as deeper thereby.* (A. L. Kroeber, 1972: xii)

Clifford Geertz, who in some aspects of his work is close both to Alfred Kroeber and Ruth Benedict, speaks in *Islam Observed* (1968, p. 19) of "a social history of the imagination." Geoffrey Gorer, who entered anthropology from the arts in the mid-1930s, had already written *Bali and Angkor* (1936) when, on the wave of success of *Africa Dances* (1935), he came to the United States in the late autumn of 1935. Many years later, when I was hesitating over some aspect of publication, he wrote to me that the most important thing that records of other societies can do is to widen the imagination about new forms of society in the future. And Gregory Bateson, when he turned to anthropology from a projected career in biology, took as his ideal Doughty's *Travels in Arabia Deserta* (1923), an ideal he did not integrate with his training as a biologist until he developed in *Naven* (1936) the idea of ethos as one way of organizing cultural materials. It is worth noting, also, that he first discussed the idea of ethos in a paper presented at the meeting of the International Congress of Anthropological and Ethnological Sciences held in London in the summer of 1934. It was a time when all of us were struggling with the question of how to present whole cultures in their full uniqueness and beauty.

THE YEARS OF RESPONSIBLE PUBLIC SERVICE

In the 1930s Ruth Benedict often chafed at the amount of energy Boas devoted to "good works" and lamented the time lost to research and writing. But as the Nazi crisis deepened in Europe and World War II approached, she who had so vigorously rejected such good works was in the end drawn into them.

Up to that time she was much more concerned with teaching and with her work with students. But even in the early 1930s she was becoming impatient with the general state of anthropology, was bored with meetings, and found little intellectual sustenance anywhere around her. In December 1932, while I was in New Guinea, she wrote me from Atlantic City describing the meetings of the American Association for the Advancement of Science, more particularly the Section H (Anthropology) sessions:

> *What a feebleminded institution these anthropological meetings turn this place into! You've forgotten probably—I had—how bad it can be. And Lowie isn't here, nor Sapir (nor Kroeber). Papa Franz is*

the one resource. It's not even any good hoping I can trump up any fellow feeling for Radcliffe-Brown. He is condescending to save all our souls, mine with the rest, and he certainly doesn't mince matters. He told me in the first three minutes that he was getting from two students "the first" two studies of American Indian social organization: Sol Tax for the Fox and [Fred] Eggan for the Hopi. . . . And [Sol] has now spent six weeks with the broken down Fox and can't even control the kinship terminology . . .(let alone knowing anything of the language). Eggan was with this year's laboratory group ("Oh, he just ignored that stupidity and went on his own way independently" R. Brown) and I said something about his having one advantage over Sol in that the society was less broken down (exogamy is completely lost in Fox). "Oh," he said, "They never had exogamy. They have a system that functions. If you must talk of broken down cultures there's Dobu. [8] That's broken down for you; they have lost the functioning of their system. But not Fox." I said mildly that it was one of the interesting things in [North American] Ethnology how many of these missionized Americanized groups had made functioning adjustments in culture. And I let it go at that.

If only he held to a high standard of achievement and required language control, intimacy with total culture, fundamental understanding of kinship, I could understand his scorn of work so far done in America. He could scorn work in broken cultures too. But to thrust this kind of work under my nose as the salvation of the world, it's sad. I asked him if he didn't think Opler's Apache Social Organization [Morris Opler, 1933] was a satisfactory study and he said, "Oh very confused as it came in first, but in the end when I'd whipped it in shape, very good, very good."—And I knew every twist and turn in the preparation of that MS: the one gap that Opler filled in—and proved I was right—on his return trip was the one I had pointed out to him after Chicago had Oked his thesis. Why not? I know my NA material and Brown doesn't. It's nothing against him, but it's silly of him to take such a line with me.

[8] When Radcliffe-Brown read Reo Fortune's first draft account of Dobu, he refused to believe in its accuracy; when, after reading the second draft, he was convinced it was accurate, he called Dobu a "pathological culture" that ought not to exist.

Perhaps you'll understand justifications in Brown's remarks that I don't see. He seemed to me impenetrably wrapped in his own conceit, and I certainly shan't feel justified in working to have him appointed at Columbia.[9] Of course my judgment may be premature. . . . I've got to be shown. As it stands, I don't think Brown is fighting for good work over against bad, but for work done by disciples over against work done by non-disciples. And that's fatal.

The Radcliffe-Brown speech comes tomorrow. I enclose the program, and I told you about it in my last letter—about my part in the "symposium." From [Fay-Cooper] Cole's activities here I gather it's to be a big "get together brothers" gesture. . . .

I wish I could know your and Reo's reaction to my impatience with Brown. I certainly don't feel like signing up with him against all other American anthropologists and nothing less, I think, would make relations endurable. I am terribly disappointed. . . . I am glad that you and Reo don't have to work just for approbation from these powers that be, but that we care to satisfy our own requirements. (AAW: 326–27)

The following day she continued her account of the meeting:

I'm reneging on Richard Tolman's Physics lecture, it's slides and I could steal out. . . . The "conference" was all a declination of combat. Cole told about the field techniques he had used to produce his invaluable study in the Philippines and Radcliffe-Brown talked about the interrelation of cultural traits. I at least—in my speech—did not have interference in my flow of language, and afterwards Papa Franz made a little speech, and [Peter] Buck put in a delightful plea to the effect that if we in authority would provide the wherewithal the field workers could perhaps live up to the requirements—but how do it on the money that was available for a piece of work.

The note they all emphasized was that the work could not be judged by the time invested. Cole advised tearing up one's first three months' note books. [Radcliffe-Brown] was stern with people who stayed short whiles and wrote books. Buck said one must stay years. You'd better dig

---

[9] At this time it was rumored that Radcliffe-Brown was a promising candidate to succeed Boas at Columbia. He was at the University of Chicago from 1931 to 1937.

*yourselves in the manner of [Malinowski] in the Trobriands and make
yourselves comfortable. It will be counted to you as virtue. Don't kill
yourselves. RB said he "required" a minimum of two years to a study.
What do you make of that? I was altogether hot under the collar.*

*RB ended on a very weak note, I thought. He rose to dispute my
point that change could be reconstructed from distribution, and he went
into detail over the t-k shift between Hawaii and [New Zealand]. "But,"
he said, "that tells us nothing about how change occurred. That chance
is provided now in Samoa where the same change is occurring today"
etc. I didn't call him publicly but afterwards I asked him what observations he would make to give us data on Samoa on how this shift occurred—(that was his point)—and he said: "Oh, but I'm not a linguist.
Let them make the tests." "But would you expect to get in the end more
than the fact that the change had occurred?" "Oh but you would have
observed it." I am quoting but I wish you were here to put sense into it.
Privately I think he's a sensationalist who gets a sense of validity only
from first hand contact.[10] But more than that is his sense of a category
of disciples and non-disciples, of course.*

*The Papa has come through the meetings very well—he hasn't been
dragged down at any time as he sometimes is even after a Columbia lecture. He made his retiring President's speech [11] on "The Aims of Anthropological Research" [Boas, 1933]—one of those close-packed meaty sum-
maries that nobody can read without a key. I'll send you a copy. It's his
testament. But nobody will ever do any shouting over it. (AAW: 327–28)*

These were the Depression years when the economic outlook everywhere was gloomy in the extreme. However, within the Department, the
Depression was experienced primarily in terms of the great difficulties of
finding any money for students to do field work and for them to live on
while they wrote up their results. Boas, who had been in Germany in the

[10] "Sensationalist" in the Jungian sense of reliance on sensation. In fact, Radcliffe-Brown
lacked sensory vividness; he could make a point in the abstract that had no objective reality
for him at all.

[11] At this meeting Boas was retiring from the presidency of the American Association for
the Advancement of Science. Early in the year he had been critically ill and only very
slowly made a recovery. It was then that possible candidates to succeed him, including
Radcliffe-Brown, began to be named in rumor.

FRANZ BOAS.

summer of 1931, was far more aware than most Americans of the deepening political crisis there and of the growing menace of Fascism. It was perhaps this concern with the political persecutions and loss of freedom in Germany and the implicit dangers for the rest of the world that skewed departmental interests away from the more immediately pressing economic issues.

Between the mid-1930s and the time of the entrance of the United States into World War II, both Boas and Ruth Benedict became actively involved in a series of battles over academic freedom that brought them into conflict not only with Stalinists but also with anti-Stalinists who periodically accused them of having Communist sympathies. During the Spanish Civil War (1936–1939) premature anti-Fascists—as they later came to be called—were not popular in the United States. However, Boas and Ruth Benedict were completely scornful of the dangers of guilt by association. Both of them thought that their personal integrity was so far above reproach that no prudence was dictated. Attacks on Boas focused especially on his association with the American Committee for Democracy and Intellectual Freedom, of which he became Chairman.

In Ruth Benedict's case the climax came in the war years in virulent attacks on a little pamphlet, "The Races of Mankind" (Benedict and Weltfish, 1943g), which was a simple exposition of scientific information about race. The specific focus of attack was data showing that during World War I northern blacks had achieved higher median scores on Army intelligence tests than southern whites, which the authors attributed to "differences in income, education, cultural advantages, and other opportunities." Owing to the controversy, the pamphlet was very widely read and discussed. It was translated into seven other languages and an educational animated cartoon was based on it.

During these years Ruth Benedict also came to devote a great deal of time to lecturing—she who still hated lecturing in public—and writing on race, on war, and on the larger issues of democracy. In discussing these matters she spoke always in her role as an anthropologist, and in this way became known far outside the small circle of her profession.

Of course, she was by no means alone in these activities. As Americans became more aware of Nazi atrocities in Europe, they often bracketed together Negroes and Jews as the social victims of prejudice, discrimination, and oppression. Many of the leading anthropologists in the United States were Jews with close ties to Europe and European scholarship. Now everything they valued in Europe was endangered, not least of all the lively intellectual and personal camaraderie in which Germans and German Jews had been drawn together in the youth and young manhood of men like Boas, Kroeber, and Lowie.

Responding to the situation as scientists, anthropologists were increasingly drawn into current controversies about problems of race. Their recognition that inheritance follows family lines and that it is not valid to speak of the "racial characteristics" of large, heterogeneous populations put them in the forefront of the battle not only against anti-Semitism but also against anti-Negro propaganda. At this time Gunnar Myrdal was carrying out his massive study on American race relations (Myrdal, 1944), and American social scientists were beginning to work intensively on Negro-white problems both in the North and in the South—as, for example, in the studies made by Allison Davis and Burleigh and Mary Gardner (1941), John Dollard (1937), Melville Herskovits (1941), and Hortense Powdermaker (1939).

BOAS' RETIREMENT: A PERIOD OF TRANSITION

In 1936 Franz Boas retired from the chairmanship of the Department. He had again fallen seriously ill, and Ruth Benedict had to take over formally responsibilities which she had carried informally for several years. In 1937, she was finally appointed Associate Professor, and in the interval between Boas' retirement and the appointment of a new chairman she was appointed acting executive officer of the Department.

Given the prevailing climate of opinion, it was believed that she could never seriously be considered as a possible successor to Boas. The Faculty of Political Science, to which Anthropology had been transferred from the Faculty of Philosophy, Anthropology, and Psychology, felt that the addition of a woman to their ranks as a full professor would lower their standing in the academic community. As a result, Ruth Benedict's appointment as Professor was not made until July 1948. Her photograph is still the only one of a woman in Fayerweather Hall's balcony room, where the portraits of all the full professors in the Faculty cover the walls.

But it might just possibly have been otherwise. After the publication of *An Anthropologist at Work* (1959), Sidney Ratner, Professor of History at Rutgers University, related to me an interesting incident that occurred while he was a research assistant in constitutional law at Columbia University in the academic year 1935–1936. In the spring of 1936, Howard Lee McBain, who was then Dean of the Graduate School, told Ratner that he planned to name Ruth Benedict chairman of the Department of Anthropology. He remarked that some university was going to have to make a woman chairman of a graduate department and that Columbia ought to be the first to do so. But Dean McBain died of a heart attack on May 7, 1936. Although Ruth Benedict had long conferences on Department affairs with him after she became acting executive officer, she never knew of this plan.

The search for a successor to Boas had begun well before his retirement. It was known that his own preferred choice was either Alfred Kroeber or Edward Sapir. But he was to have neither one. We soon learned that the most likely candidates were W. Lloyd Warner and Ralph Linton. Ironically, it was because we both felt that Linton's approach was so compatible with Ruth Benedict's that she favored Lloyd Warner, whose approach would have complemented hers. However, Linton was invited to Columbia as Visiting Professor in the autumn of 1937, and he very soon received the permanent appointment as chairman. He learned that Ruth had not supported his candidacy and he never forgave her.

Although Boas remained as Professor Emeritus and came in once or twice a week until his death in December 1942, the Department was soon radically transformed. The new situation was made very difficult for Ruth Benedict both because of her long years of association with Boas— and her continuing work with him on causes outside the Department— and because of the strained relationship with Linton.

For several years she had directed a series of field studies among American Indian groups and had been very excited by the possibilities presented by the analysis of these field materials. In the end, however, she turned over to Ralph Linton the task of drawing this work together, and the book that resulted, *Acculturation in Seven American Indian Tribes* (1940), was edited by Linton.

But she continued to work with her students. In 1936, Stanley Benedict died and left her substantially better off. She used her increased means to facilitate her students' work. In this she followed, in part, the pattern that had been set by Elsie Clews Parsons, from which she had benefited in her own early years in anthropology.

Then, following the field laboratory trip to the Blackfoot in the summer of 1939, she took a year's sabbatical leave, which she spent in California near her mother and her sister. She devoted this year to the writing of *Race: Science and Politics* (1940b) as a major contribution to the fight for freedom.

Soon after her return to Columbia in the autumn of 1940, she was offered the Anna Shaw Memorial Lectureship at Bryn Mawr College for the spring of 1941. Although it was a signal honor, she had great difficulty in arranging for the necessary semester's leave of absence. At Bryn Mawr she lectured on synergy, a concept that initially interested her enormously. Essentially, it consisted of an analysis of the way in which social institutions can combine to produce harmonious and energizing effects. She was still lecturing on the subject at Columbia in 1946, but unfortunately only a few notes survive (Maslow and Honigmann, 1970).

THE WAR YEARS

In the autumn of 1939, while Ruth Benedict was in California, a small group (including, among others, Gregory Bateson, Eliot D. Chapple, Lawrence K. Frank, and myself) came together in the Committee for National Morale, organized by Arthur Upham Pope, to consider ways in which the sciences of anthropology and psychology, in particular, could be applied to the problems of morale building in wartime, for it was already clear to us that the United States could not long stand apart from the war. In this committee we began to develop methods of interviewing highly educated members of other cultures on their own lives as a way of deriving data on basic themes relevant to their own culture.

Initially Ruth Benedict was not very much interested in these activities. By 1941, however, she was drawn into other activities related to the war situation. When the Committee on Food Habits of the National Research Council was set up by M. L. Wilson, the Director of Extension in the Department of Agriculture and Chairman of the Federal Interdepartmental Nutrition Coordinating Committee, she was asked to become a member. The Committee was given the responsibility of working on cultural change in relation to food habits and nutrition on a national scale. When it was decided, late in the year, that the Committee needed an executive secretary, she was asked to recruit me. She told me of the invitation to join the Committee on Food Habits while I was at a conference on the afternoon of the attack on Pearl Harbor. I went to Washington early in 1942. Ruth Benedict continued as a member of the Committee and came to Washington periodically to attend its meetings.

In 1941 Lawrence K. Frank, Gregory Bateson, and I formed another small voluntary organization, which was known first as the Council for Intercultural Relations and later as the Institute for Intercultural Studies. Ruth Benedict became a founding member. Through this organization we continued to pursue our research on what eventually was called "national character." Slowly Ruth Benedict became involved in the work we were doing. She wrote a few brief memoranda based on interviews with specialists—one on the way in which consensus was reached in communication between rural gentry and peasants in China and another contrasting attitudes toward social work in Denmark and Norway.

One of the most notable studies made at this time was a memorandum on the Japanese, prepared by Geoffrey Gorer, based on interviews with missionaries and others who had lived in Japan and on analyses of literature on Japan. (Only some portions of this study have been published; see Gorer [1943].) Gorer completed the memorandum while he was still at Yale. Soon afterward, in the spring of 1942, he went to Washington to work in the Office of War Information. When he moved on to the British Embassy wartime staff, he nominated Ruth Benedict to replace him.

She accepted and in mid-1943 moved to Washington. There she lived with Ruth Valentine, a clinical psychologist, who was one of her close California friends. At the Office of War Information she was asked to prepare memoranda on both European and Asian cultures—on problems related to nations with which the United States was involved because they were active allies, enemies, or countries occupied by the enemy. She worked, of course, inside a high security clearance, a clearance that was initially complicated by the furor in Congress over the little pamphlet, "The Races of Mankind" (Benedict and Weltfish, 1943g), which the Navy had accepted with enthusiasm but which the Army had rejected.

The office in which she worked was large and noisy. Nevertheless she managed to insulate herself from the gossip, the endless discussions, and the innumerable conferences that take up so much time and energy in government agencies. Uninterested in the infighting that so often went on around her, she went placidly about her own tasks. For once her deafness was an advantage, as it gave her an area of privacy in her small working space.

By 1943 there were a large number of anthropologists in various government agencies in Washington. Several of us who were interested in the problems of studying national character and in developing techniques for research on cultures at a distance continued to meet as a small, informal, closely communicating group to review the work we were doing—as far as this was possible within wartime security restrictions—and to make plans.

It was to this small group that Ruth Benedict brought her first extended work, a study on Rumania (1943d). In setting up this study she had received help from Philip Mosely, who had done field research in that country and was in touch with Rumanians in the United States. The

58

Rumanian study set the pattern for her later work on Thailand (1943e), on various European cultures—German, Dutch, Belgian, Polish—and, with increasing concentration as the war continued, on Japan.

Those of us who had initially developed methods for work on national character in complex, highly literate cultures relied about equally on anthropological and psychoanalytic insights as we strove to find central themes around which programs could be built. But Ruth Benedict, who never worked happily with psychoanalytic concepts or, indeed, within the confines of any specifically psychological theory, made no attempt to master this approach. She had slowly come to accept the idea that an understanding of childrearing methods would amplify her own chosen way of describing cultural configurations. However, although she read other people's work with sympathetic interest, she did not adopt their research methods.

In the Office of War Information she developed her own style of approach to this new kind of anthropological study of culture at a distance, in which published materials were integrated with interview data to gain an understanding of high literate cultures. Her long experience in working with students, laboriously going over and over a student's unorganized notes and half-comprehended impressions, had given her a basic technique for getting at cultural data through the medium of a second person. Her training in English literature and her intensive reading gave her a disciplined and highly sophisticated approach to published materials. And her penchant for building up a picture from fragmentary data came into play in a new way in bringing these very diverse and uneven source materials together in a significant relationship.

In carrying out these studies she had funds to employ younger anthropologists as interviewers. She herself also worked with informants. In the course of her researches on European, especially Eastern European, cultures, she became impressed with the importance of distinguishing the versions of different European cultures as represented by Jews, who constituted a large proportion of her best informants, and as represented by other sectors of the same national cultures. She also worked on extracting cultural regularities from a very miscellaneous assortment of literary sources—history, travel accounts, plays, and novels—and from a variety of sources on current wartime behavior.

As the locus of her research shifted from Europe to Japan, her own situation also changed. Her studies of European cultures were carried out within a well-known area. The sources she used were in familiar languages—German, French, Dutch, etc.—and she could place her special studies within a framework of a solid knowledge of European history, politics, and literature. The Far East, in contrast, was *terra incognita*. Before coming to Washington she had done some work on Chinese culture in connection with studies going on at Columbia and had written the brief but important memorandum on consensus in rural China. For the Office of War Information she had prepared the memorandum on Thai culture. But Japan presented a vast canvas and work on this culture, of which she had no previous knowledge, was a formidable undertaking.

She had already demonstrated in her European studies that an anthropologist, using anthropological techniques of interviewing and analysis, could make a considerable addition to the contributions of the traditional experts—historians, political scientists, economists, and areal specialists. Initially it had not been easy to convince these specialists, who felt that they "knew" Europe. But when it came to Japanese culture, with which they were unfamiliar, many of the European-trained specialists were much more willing to admit an anthropologist to the team. However, the Far East was also a field in which "old China hands" had had their way for a very long time. There were so few of them and they commanded knowledge in an area where almost everyone else was ignorant. But she had the distinct advantage in that, in her work on Japan, she had anthropological colleagues—Geoffrey Gorer, Gregory Bateson, Clyde Kluckhohn, and Alexander Leighton—who were carrying on related studies. In addition, psychologists and psychiatrists were applying, and developing further, the new methods for the study of national character in work on Japan.

As in her European studies, she had funds for employing younger interviewers to supplement her own work with informants. Also, in addition to a very rich assortment of literary materials, she had access to contemporary films. In the late 1930s the Japanese had produced a series of films for propaganda use both within Japan and in other Asian countries. Certain of these, which had become available for research, were fascinating documents on cultural themes officially fostered in wartime Japan.

Counterpointing these were other sources, such as the captured diaries of Japanese soldiers. These materials and her analyses of them were all bound by security restrictions.

Within the Office of War Information she was left relatively free to work as she liked. In part this was owing to the fact that the methods of anthropology were unfamiliar to most of her colleagues. But to a greater extent her freedom to work as she chose was a by-product of her approach. Her treatment of culture, with its rounded and sophisticated presentation, evoked no psychological concepts to disturb the reader—as did the responses aroused in bureaucrats and social scientists alike by theoretical references to breast feeding or toilet training. Instead, her presentation invited acceptance and a sense of illumination.

The fact that she was not involved in any of the current psychological controversies was in itself an attraction. She was, however, invited to give a series of lectures under the auspices of the Washington School of Psychiatry. These lectures drew a very wide audience of those from all over the country who were doing war work in Washington and, in turn, brought her a new and delighted reading audience.

At the end of the war, in the summer of 1945, she was invited by the military to go to Germany to study occupation problems. This was an exciting prospect as, during the first uneasy months of military occupation, few civilians and almost no women were permitted to enter the American zone. But when she was given a routine physical examination, the trip was vetoed. For several years the violent sick headaches that had plagued her younger days had been replaced by sudden, inexplicable attacks of extreme dizziness, and the doctors also worried about her heart. She was extremely disappointed. After these years of working intensively on cultures viewed from a distance, she was very anxious to look again at Europe, where she had not been since 1926. She longed especially to have a glimpse of countries in Eastern Europe which she had never visited.

With Europe ruled out, she decided to write a book on Japan. For this purpose she continued her wartime leave from Columbia University through the 1945–1946 academic year and went to California to write *The Chrysanthemum and the Sword* (1946a).

In her research on Japanese culture she had been tremendously impressed by the capacity of the Japanese at a crucial turning point to take a new stand and to enter wholly into the new situation. This capacity was demonstrated by the willingness of Japanese servicemen, once they had been captured, to cooperate with the American armed forces as well as by the deep sincerity of those of the American-born Japanese who elected to be loyal to the United States. What they had learned was the practice of loyal participation rather than devotion to a specific object of loyalty.

It was with this in mind that she concluded *The Chrysanthemum and the Sword* on a note of hope and warning:

> *Any European or Asiatic country which is not arming during the next decade will have a potential advantage over the countries which are arming, for its wealth can be used to build a healthy and prosperous economy. In the United States we hardly take this situation into account in our Asiatic and European policies, for we know that we would not be impoverished in this country by expensive programs of national defense. Our country was not devastated. We are not primarily an agricultural country. Our crucial problem is industrial overproduction. We have perfected mass production and mechanical equipment until our population cannot find employment unless we set in motion great programs of armament or of luxury production or of welfare and research services. The need for profitable investment of capital is also acute. This situation is quite different outside the United States. It is different even in Western Europe. In spite of all demands for reparations, a Germany which is not allowed to rearm could in a decade or so have laid the foundations of a sound and prosperous economy which would be impossible in France if her policy is to build up great military power. Japan could make the most of a similar advantage over China. Militarization is a current goal in China and her ambitions are supported by the United States. Japan, if she does not include militarization in her budget, can, if she will, provide for her own prosperity before many years, and she could make herself indispensable in the commerce of the East. She could base her economy on the profits of peace and raise the standard of living of her people. Such a peaceful Japan could attain a place of honor among the nations of the world, and the United States*

could be of great assistance if it continued to use its influence in support of such a program.

What the United States cannot do—what no outside nation could do—is to create by fiat a free, democratic Japan. It has never worked in any dominated country. No foreigner can decree, for a people who have not his habits and assumptions, a manner of life after his own image. The Japanese cannot be legislated into accepting the authority of elected persons and ignoring 'proper station' as it is set up in their hierarchal system. They cannot be legislated into adopting the free and easy human contacts to which we are accustomed in the United States, the imperative demand to be independent, the passion each individual has to choose his own mate, his own job, the house he will live in and the obligations he will assume. The Japanese themselves, however, are quite articulate about changes in this direction which they regard as necessary. Their public men have said since VJ-Day that Japan must encourage its men and women to live their own lives and to trust their own consciences. They do not say so, of course, but any Japanese understands that they are questioning the rôle of 'shame' (haji) in Japan, and that they hope for a new growth of freedom among their countrymen: freedom from fear of the criticism and ostracism of 'the world.'

For social pressures in Japan, no matter how voluntarily embraced, ask too much of the individual. They require him to conceal his emotions, to give up his desires, and to stand as the exposed representative of a family, an organization or a nation. The Japanese have shown that they can take all the self-discipline such a course requires. But the weight upon them is extremely heavy. They have to repress too much for their own good. Fearing to venture upon a life which is less costly to their psyches, they have been led by militarists upon a course where the costs pile up interminably. Having paid so high a price, they became self-righteous and have been contemptuous of people with a less demanding ethic.

The Japanese have taken the first great step toward social change by identifying aggressive warfare as an 'error' and a lost cause. They hope to buy their passage back to a respected place among peaceful nations. It will have to be a peaceful world. If Russia and the United States

63

spend the coming years in arming for attack, Japan will use her know-how to fight in that war. But to admit that certainty does not call in question the inherent possibility of a peaceful Japan. Japan's motivations are situational. She will seek her place within a world at peace if circumstances permit. If not, within a world organized as an armed camp.

At present the Japanese know militarism as a light that failed. They will watch to see whether it has also failed in other nations of the world. If it has not, Japan can relight her own warlike ardor and show how well she can contribute. If it has failed elsewhere, Japan can set herself to prove how well she has learned the lesson that imperialistic dynastic enterprises are no road to honor. (pp. 313–16)

The contemporary reader is immediately struck by the absence of any reference to the atomic bomb and the Japanese response to the catastrophe. In 1946, the significance of the impact of Hiroshima on Japanese thinking had not yet penetrated American consciousness. *The Chrysanthemum and the Sword* is, in fact, completely related to Japanese culture as Ruth Benedict had come to understand it through her wartime studies.

In writing this book she had at her disposal not only her own research but also the initial work done on Japan by Geoffrey Gorer (1943) and Gregory Bateson, the later work of Clyde Kluckhohn and Alexander Leighton, and materials made available through the training and research sections of the Office of Strategic Services. Many of these sources were classified and could not be acknowledged in the preface to the book. But while she drew on earlier formulations by others, the integration of the material was uniquely her own.

It is the book she cared more about than any other she had written. The most complex expression of her work as an anthropologist, it is also the work in which she herself felt she was most fully committed and wholly engaged. The book itself has become a classic. It was almost immediately translated into Japanese and was very widely discussed in Japan.[12] Her anthropological approach, the beauty of her writing, and

[12] Bennett and Nagai (1953), in their analysis of the Japanese response to the book, refer to the discussion in *Minzokugaku Kenkyu* (The Japanese Journal of Ethnology), Special Issue on *The Chrysanthemum and the Sword* (14, no. 4, Tokyo, 1949). Sales of some 124,000

the breadth of her humanity ensure its enduring value. A pioneering work in its scope, it continues to stimulate students of Japanese culture, both Japanese fieldworkers and fieldworkers from other parts of the world.

Like most work done on the study of cultures at a distance, *The Chrysanthemum and the Sword* represents a piece of research carried out under the pressure of an urgent need to understand a people with whom, at the time, those by whom the research was being done could not communicate directly and whose culture could not be studied in their own country. No fieldworker would ever choose to do research under these circumstances. But the book that came out of this work on Japan remains as a beautiful demonstration of the way in which a belief in the wholeness of a culture makes possible the integration of fragmented, scattered, and disparate materials in a coherent and complex portrait of the culture.

RESEARCH IN CONTEMPORARY CULTURES

In the fall of 1946 Ruth Benedict returned to Columbia, but without a great deal of enthusiasm. The ties to her sister, her sister's children, her mother, and her California friends always made her long visits to California enjoyable. But New York was her home and she felt very strongly her responsibility for her students at Columbia. However, the years since Boas' retirement and his death in 1942 had not been easy ones and the period of wartime work in Washington had only provided a respite from the difficulties within the Department and in relations with the university administration. In 1946, Ralph Linton accepted an appointment as Sterling Professor of Anthropology at Yale University, but the appointment of Julian Steward to succeed him as professor (although not as chairman of the Department) at Columbia meant neither sympathy nor support for the kind of teaching and the kind of research in which she was interested. And she was still an associate professor without the means or the influence to provide well for her students.

In June 1946, she was given the Annual Achievement Award of the American Association of University Women. Her acceptance speech reflects both her concern for her students—including those who were com-

---

copies of the Japanese editions in 1973 indicate the continuing interest in this book among readers in Japan.

ing to Columbia from other countries to study under her—and her hopes and plans for the future:

. . . I feel that my thanks will be best expressed by describing to you the kind of work which your award will help to carry on.

Three years ago I was asked to come to Washington to help in the war effort, and I am only now returning to Columbia University this fall. I was asked when I came to the Office of War Information to undertake research on civilized nations, both enemy and occupied. I was asked to state in an anthropologist's fashion the problems to be investigated in order to answer the recurring problems with which we were faced, and to use in so far as possible familiar anthropological techniques for solving them. These ways of stating problems of human behavior and these techniques for solving them had been worked out, for several decades, in anthropological studies of small tribes, usually without written language, whose traditional ways of conducting life owed very little indeed to the influences of Western civilization. . . .

I had believed for a long time before the war that the same kind of research could help us to understand civilized nations. I believed that by serious study of learned cultural behavior we could achieve a better international understanding and make fewer mistakes in international communication. Many writers have asked the question of what makes the United States a nation of Americans and France a nation of Frenchmen and China a nation of Chinese, but the answers have either been impressionistic or they have been narrowly historical, economic, or political. The data which the anthropologist finds necessary in order to answer such a question even for a simple primitive tribe were lacking for European nations. They were either unrecorded or they were scattered in a thousand surveys and novels. In my work during the war I had to make the best of a difficult situation. I could not observe daily behavior on the spot in these nations, nor send a trained student. There were, however, plenty of nationals from all parts of the world in this country, and in face-to-face contact and conversation I was able to gather a great deal of material and comment which was essential to my studies.

I worked on the nations of Asia a great part of the time, and my work on Japan I have written up in a book, The Chrysanthemum and the

Sword: Patterns of Japanese Culture, *which will be published this fall.*
But it is for continued work of this kind in understanding the nations of
Europe that I shall use the award you have given me. Next year I shall
have a work seminar at Columbia University for students of European
background. Some will be holders of fellowships who are in this country
to finish their education and will be returning to their home countries
immediately. Some will be men and women of European origin who
have lived in the United States for some years. I shall give them train-
ing in methods of study by arranging opportunities for them to observe
American life and having them report on their observations. Their point
of view is important in understanding how the United States looks to
outsiders, and training will help them to document their impressions or
will lead them possibly to revise or rephrase their judgments. They will
also report on their own experiences in their native land, and the object
of the training will be to teach them techniques of adequate statement
and documentation of the conduct of life in their home country.

Such materials must be supplemented later by field work on the spot
in the nations selected, but I believe that such a seminar as I have de-
scribed can be an important contribution. In such a give and take of re-
actions, accompanied always by training in what satisfactory documen-
tation consists of, I believe we can try out in little some of the problems
which face the United Nations. I have the faith of a scientist that be-
havior, no matter how unfamiliar to us, is understandable if the prob-
lem is stated so that it can be answered by investigation and if it is then
studied by technically suitable methods. And I have the faith of a
humanist in the advantages of mutual understanding among men.

The money award you have given me will go farther in this research
than you perhaps think. Every research worker, but especially one in the
social sciences, knows how certain opportunities must usually be passed
by because in the original arrangements for the research so much is nec-
essarily unforeseen. He knows too how often the university or the foun-
dation may be willing to make an appropriation for one part of the work
and not for another; it may be possible to swing the collection of data
and then be stymied when it comes to provisions for students to enable
them to write up their material. In making this award you have put
money at my disposal which has no strings attached to it except that it

67

shall be used to further the work. I can use it at all those places which are otherwise unprovided for or which I cannot foresee before the moment arises. At each such emergency, I shall feel fresh gratitude to the American Association of University Women which has trusted me with this award. You will have an intimate part in the research as it proceeds. (AAW: 430–32)

So we had come full circle. She whom we had had to persuade that the study of culture at a distance could be rewarding was now prepared to make the central focus of her teaching just such studies of high civilizations—not excluding studies of American culture by foreign students—so that we could better learn "how the United States looks to outsiders." In her thinking she had absorbed the possibility of large research plans which had characterized Boas' work from the time of the Jesup North Pacific Expedition (1897–1902) and which Ruth Benedict had hoped to carry further through the American Indian studies she had inaugurated at Columbia not long before the war.

However, she did not after all have to support her studies of European cultures with the slender resources of the award—twenty-five hundred dollars—given by the American Association of University Women. Immediately after the war the Office of Naval Research developed a plan to organize studies in human resources, using money already appropriated for warfare to build for an enduring peace. In the spring of 1946, Ruth Benedict tantalized us with the announcement that she knew where to obtain $100,000 in research funds. At first none of us believed her; it seemed to us an extravagant sum. But it was a fact. She had been asked to become a member of the Committee on Research of the Office of Naval Research, and each member was invited to submit a proposal for a project.

Negotiations got under way. In the midst of the process of getting the contract signed there was a last effort to sabotage her obtaining the grant. She had been nominated for the presidency of the American Anthropological Association, but at the annual meeting the committee that was concerned with carrying out a reorganization of the Association proposed, ingeniously, that Ralph Linton should continue as president for an extended period until the new constitution came into effect. This would

RUTH BENEDICT IN THE POSTWAR YEARS OF RECOGNITION.

have barred Ruth Benedict from the presidency and quite possibly would have discredited the delicate negotiations still under way with the Office of Naval Research. Fortunately, this move was successfully opposed. She was elected President of the American Anthropological Association (1946–47), and the project, Columbia University Research in Contemporary Cultures, was inaugurated in the spring of 1947. And finally, in 1948, she was appointed a full professor at Columbia.

Initially the project presented massive difficulties. Columbia University, where the project was to be located, was unwilling to provide any space. As a result it was necessary to borrow space all over the city—in the Kips Bay-Yorkville District Health Center, in the Office of the Cultural Counselor to the French Embassy, and in other temporary locations. The research groups on each culture, as they were formed, met, for the most part, in the homes of members. With great generosity the Viking Fund (which, in 1951, became the Wenner-Gren Foundation for Anthropological Research) offered us a meeting room for monthly seminars, the only place where all the members of the project could gather at one time. Eventually the project acquired office space in the old—and condemned—building of the Columbia University Medical School, but this was long in coming and provided no room for holding meetings.

But we were optimistic. The funds available seemed vast. In the end, the cost of the whole project was to run to a quarter of a million dollars, which was, in fact, a modest sum for a complex research program that lasted for four years (1947–1951) and that involved more than 120 participants in work on seven cultures. These participants "represented fourteen disciplines, sixteen nationalities, and varied in age from the early twenties to the late fifties and in level of training from occasional very gifted undergraduates to senior members of their profession with experience in half a dozen cultures" (Mead and Metraux, 1953, p. 6).

In making plans for the organization of the project we tried to realize as many as possible of our earlier daydreams. There was to be a loose framework within which members of different disciplines could work together on shared materials. There was to be a place for people with unusual talents and idiosyncratic working habits, people who had managed to survive during the war years because their services were so badly needed but who fitted very unreadily into any bureaucratic structure.

There was to be a place for graduate students and others who needed supplementary grants, a place for some participants to work full time and for volunteers who had their own income resources. The one basic requirement was that each person who joined the project did so out of intrinsic interest in the work itself.

To ensure the sharing of all materials we arranged for adequate typing help for those who could not type their own work. The duplicating machines that later made the sharing of materials so much easier were not yet available. In the beginning all reports were typed in four line-numbered copies. Mindful of the hundreds of hours wastefully consumed in the rewriting and reorganization of poorly written work an editor, Elizabeth Herzog, was provided to help those who needed assistance with the preparation and editing of reports.

The organization was non-hierarchical. On the organizational chart the project itself occupied the central position. It was necessary, of course, to connect Ruth Benedict, as director, both to Columbia University and to the Office of Naval Research. But within the project most participants played at least two roles, one carrying more and the other less responsibility, within different research groups. This meant both that almost no one held a single fixed position in the group at large and that most members participated simultaneously in research on two cultures. The exceptions were a few participants who joined the project out of a very specific interest in research on their own culture. And to keep the whole group involved in the process of learning, everyone, including the office staff, took part in the project seminars at which ongoing work was presented and discussed.

No clearances were required for participation in the project and there were strict provisions that all work was to be unclassified and that no "secret" materials were to be used. These provisions were essential to win and hold the trust of participants, many of whom had experienced the difficulties and ambiguities of working within wartime security regulations. But the very openness of the whole program meant that the identity of every informant had to be scrupulously protected. Each active researcher coded his or her own informants, and only these code numbers—never the names of informants—were entered in the project files.

RESEARCH IN CONTEMPORARY CULTURES

Structure of a Non-Hierarchical Organization 1947–1951

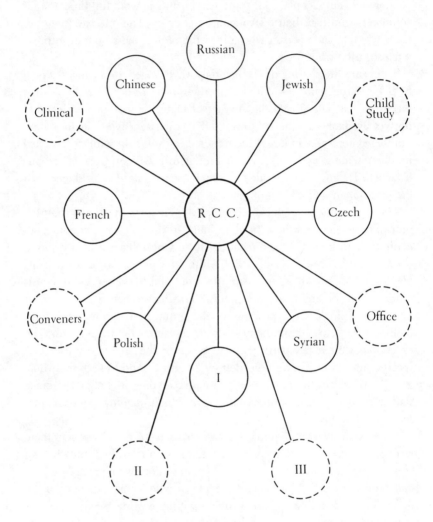

KEY TO CHART

Central Circle: General Seminar

Closed Circles: Research groups on seven cultures; and I—Individual exploration

Open Circles: Cross-cutting Groups; and II—Cross-cultural consultants
III—Professor Benedict's European Seminar at Columbia University

SOURCE: Mead and Metraux (1953), p. 90.

If we could keep the kind of knowledge that we were developing in a form that was useful to peace and prevent it from becoming classified and specialized to any purpose of psychological warfare, we believed we could work with good conscience. Our experience with the different uses of anthropological and psychological techniques in wartime had convinced us that psychological warfare always in the long run backfired on the user. But we were equally convinced that the responsible application of anthropological knowledge had made important contributions, for example, to the decision not to insist on the abdication of the Japanese emperor as a prime condition for ending the war in the Pacific, to the conduct of the postwar occupation in Europe and in the Pacific, to reconstruction abroad, and not least, to morale at home. Now we reasoned that whatever the postwar political alignments might be, knowledge about ourselves and other countries was essential. Wartime experience had given us a more sophisticated sense of the anthropologist's responsibilities. Building on this we set to work.

In spite of ample funds and gradually improving facilities, the project was a very difficult one to administer. Ruth Benedict's office at Columbia and mine at the American Museum of Natural History absorbed part of the administration. But the scattering of office space and meeting places made work difficult and communication time-consuming. Ruth Valentine came back from California to take over part of the administrative work, and this somewhat eased the burden Ruth Benedict had to carry.

However, the organizational style was congenial to Ruth Bendict, and this outweighed the difficulties. Each participant was given individual responsibility, and each person who became a member of the group was selected for who he or she was—not because we needed a statistician, or a specialist in French history, or a demographer. People elected to join us, and those who could gave their time and skills without pay. This hospitality and openness pleased Ruth and contributed greatly to the common spirit of enthusiasm that rapidly developed among the group as a whole.

But the continual administrative struggle, the lack of support from the Department at Columbia, and the recurrently grudging character of the University administration wearied her. Although she acted also as convener of the Czech group, she had very little time to do any original work. Evenings in which we used to discuss poetry and the novelistic aspects of real life were now filled with petty details. She often looked very tired.

In the spring of 1948 it became clear that the project, in spite of its financial resources, had already become overextended. In search of a solution she began negotiations with RAND for a set of Russian studies (Mead, 1951) and with the Carnegie Foundation for an advance on a book that was to be based on the project research. This advance was withdrawn after Ruth Benedict's death.

Then in May 1948 she was invited to take part in a seminar sponsored by UNESCO that was to be held in Podebrady, Czechoslavakia. This would require no hampering physical examination and it would give her the coveted chance to visit Europe. She wanted terribly to go—to see with her own eyes Czechoslovakia, Poland, Holland, and Belgium, countries she had treated with such imaginative realism from a distance. Yet she wondered: Was it wise, in the middle of a big project, to take the risk? She had always backed up us, her students, in any necessary risk we proposed to take in carrying out our work. Now we said: Go!

The summer was all she hoped it would be. The UNESCO seminar was a great success. Friends who met her later in various places in Europe reported her delight over finding out how accurate her work had been—over her discovery that Poles and Czechs, Dutch and Belgians actually did behave as her studies had informed her they did.

But her strength failed. Two days after she returned, before she was again burdened by details of the project, she suffered a coronary thrombosis. She died five days later, on September 17. It was a comfort to those who, like her sister Margery, had always been shocked by Ruth's positive attitude toward the peace that is death that she was a good patient to the end. When she was taken to the hospital and was told that she must rest and not worry, she smiled and said, "My friends will take care of everything."

Research in Contemporary Cultures, which was her last major contribution to anthropology, continued. This project—as well as others for which it provided a model—fully integrated her scientific and humanistic approaches to culture. In this sense the research design, unifying themes that had been central in Ruth Benedict's life, also expressed her conception of how anthropology can best contribute to our understanding of high cultures. She herself had said:

> *I have the faith of a scientist that behavior, no matter how unfamiliar to us, is understandable if the problem is stated so that it can be answered by investigation and if it is then studied by technically suitable methods. And I have the faith of a humanist in the advantages of mutual understanding among men.* (AAW: 431)

Eucharist

Light the more given is the more denied.
Though you go seeking by the naked seas,
Each cliff etched visible and all the waves
Pluming themselves with sunlight, of this pride
Light makes her sophistries.

You are not like to find her, being fed
Always with that she shines on. Only those
Storm-driven down the dark, see light arise,
Her body broken for their rainbow bread
At late and shipwrecked close.

Ruth Benedict

REFERENCES *

Alexander, Franz, and Helen Ross, eds. 1952. *Dynamic Psychiatry.* Chicago: University of Chicago Press.

Barnouw, Victor. 1949. Ruth Benedict: Apollonian and Dionysian. *University of Toronto Quarterly* 18:241–53.

———. 1957. The Amiable Side of *Patterns of Culture. American Anthropologist* 59:532–35.

Bateson, Gregory. 1936. *Naven.* Cambridge: University Press. 2d ed., 1958, Stanford: Stanford University Press.

Bennett, John W., and Michio Nagai. 1953. The Japanese Critique of the Methodology of Benedict's *The Chrysanthemum and the Sword. American Anthropologist* 55:404–11.

Boas, Franz. 1932. The Aims of Anthropological Research. *Science* 76:605–13.

———, ed. 1938. *General Anthropology.* Boston and New York: Heath.

Bunzel, Ruth. 1929. *The Pueblo Potter: A Study of Creative Imagination in Primitive Art.* Columbia University Contributions to Anthropology, No. 8. New York: Columbia University Press. Reprinted 1972, New York: Dover.

Davis, Allison, Burleigh Gardner, and Mary Gardner. 1941. *Deep South.* Chicago: University of Chicago Press.

Dollard, John. 1937. *Caste and Class in a Southern Town.* New York: Harper. 3d ed., 1957, Garden City, New York: Doubleday.

Doughty, Charles M. 1923. *Travels in Arabia Deserta,* 3d ed. London: Cape and the Medici Society. First published 1888.

Fortune, Reo F. 1932. *Sorcerers of Dobu.* New York: Dutton. Rev. ed., 1963.

Geertz, Clifford. 1968. *Islam Observed: Religious Development in Morocco and Indonesia.* New Haven: Yale University Press.

Goldenweiser, Alexander A. 1910. Totemism, an Analytical Study. *Journal of American Folk-Lore* 23:179–293.

———. 1922. *Early Civilization.* New York: Knopf.

Goldfrank, Esther S. 1945. *Changing Configurations in the Social Organization of a Blackfoot Tribe during the Reserve Period (The Blood of Alberta).* Monographs of the American Ethnological Society, No. 8. New York: Augustin.

Goldman, Irving. 1937. The Zuni Indians of New Mexico. In *Cooperation and Competition among Primitive Peoples,* ed. Margaret Mead, pp. 313–53. New York: McGraw-Hill. Rev. ed., 1961, Boston: Beacon Press.

Gorer, Geoffrey. 1935. *Africa Dances.* London: Faber. Rev. ed., 1949, London: Lehmann.

———. 1936. *Bali and Angkor.* London: Michael Joseph.

———. 1943. Themes in Japanese Culture. *Transactions,* The New York Academy of Sciences, Ser. 2, 5:106–24.

Herskovits, Melville J. 1926. The Cattle Complex in East Africa. *Memoirs of the American Anthropological Association,* No. 16.

———. 1941. *The Myth of the Negro Past.* New York: Harper.

———. 1953. *Franz Boas: The Science of Man in the Making.* New York: Scribner's.

* FOR REFERENCES to the work of Ruth Benedict, see Selected Bibliography below, pp. 177–80.

Jung, C. G. 1923. *Psychological Types*, trans. H. G. Baynes. New York: Harcourt, Brace.

Kroeber, Alfred L. 1923. *Anthropology*. New York: Harcourt, Brace.

———. 1972. *More Mohave Myths*. University of California Publications in Anthropological Records, No. 27. Berkeley and Los Angeles: University of California Press.

Kroeber, Theodora. 1970. *Alfred Kroeber: A Personal Configuration*. Berkeley and Los Angeles: University of California Press.

Li An-che. 1937. Zuni: Some Observations and Queries. *American Anthropologist* 39:63–76.

Linton, Ralph, ed. 1940. *Acculturation in Seven American Indian Tribes*. New York: Appleton-Century.

Lowie, Robert H. 1920. *Primitive Society*. New York: Boni and Liveright.

Maslow, Abraham H., and John J. Honigmann. 1970. Synergy: Some Notes of Ruth Benedict. *American Anthropologist* 72:320–33.

Mead, Margaret. 1928. *An Inquiry into the Question of Cultural Stability in Polynesia*. Columbia University Contributions to Anthropology, No. 9. New York: Columbia University Press.

———. 1930. Social Organization in Manu'a. *Bernice P. Bishop Museum Bulletin*, No. 76. Honolulu. 2d ed., 1969.

———, ed. 1937. *Cooperation and Competition among Primitive Peoples*. New York: McGraw-Hill. Rev. ed., 1961, Boston: Beacon Press.

———. 1951. *Soviet Attitudes toward Authority*. New York: McGraw-Hill. Reprinted 1955, New York: Morrow, and 1966, New York: Schocken.

———. 1959. *An Anthropologist at Work: Writings of Ruth Benedict*. Boston: Houghton Mifflin. Paperback edition, 1973, New York: Avon.

———, and Rhoda Metraux, eds. 1953. *The Study of Culture at a Distance*. Chicago: University of Chicago Press.

Minzokugaku Kenkyu 14, no. 4 (The Japanese Journal of Ethnology). 1949. Special Issue on *The Chrysanthemum and the Sword* (Tokyo).

Myrdal, Gunnar. 1944. *An American Dilemma*, 2 vols. New York: Harper.

Opler, Morris. 1933. An Analysis of Mescalero and Chiricahua Apache Social Organization in the Light of Their Systems of Relationship. Ph.D. dissertation, Department of Anthropology, University of Chicago.

Pandey, Triloki Nath. 1972. Anthropologists at Zuni. *Proceedings of the American Philosophical Society*, No. 116, pp. 321–37.

Powdermaker, Hortense. 1939. *After Freedom*. New York: Viking.

Rivers, W. H. R. 1923. *Conflict and Dream*. London: Routledge.

Seligman, C. G. 1923. Anthropology and Psychology: A Study of Some Points of Contact. *Journal of the Royal Athropological Institute* 54:13.

Thomas, W. L. Jr., ed. 1955. *Yearbook of Anthropology*. New York: Wenner-Gren Foundation for Anthropological Research.

Waterman, T. T. 1914. The Exploratory Element in the Folk-Tales of the North-American Indians. *Journal of American Folk-Lore* 27:1–54.

Wissler, Clark. 1929. *An Introduction to Social Anthropology*. New York: Holt.

Selected Papers

Introduction

✤ The choice of articles for presentation here has been guided by several considerations. Certain articles, such as "Anthropology and the Abnormal" (1934a) and "Continuities and Discontinuities in Cultural Conditioning" (1938a), have been widely reprinted in anthologies and so they are omitted here. Certain other articles seem essential.

"Configurations of Cultural in North America" (1932a) is the most complete expression of her theoretical position preceding her book *Patterns of Culture* (1934b). "Magic" (1933a), one of several articles she prepared for the old *Encyclopedia of the Social Sciences*, exemplifies both the breadth of her scholarship and her ability to cut through conflicting viewpoints sharply and concisely on a subject about which, today, there is again considerable confusion. *Zuni Mythology* (1935a) represents her most massive field work, and the Introduction raises many problems with which folklorists have not yet come to terms. "Primitive Freedom" (1942b) is one of the best examples of the way in which she used primitive materials in a sophisticated commentary on significant contemporary issues. "Self-Discipline in Japanese Culture," taken from *The Chrysanthemum and the Sword* (1946a), is an example of her capacity to integrate cultural materials on a culture to which she had no direct access. "The Study of Cultural Patterns in European Nations" (1946c) states concisely her plan to continue studies begun during World War II, a plan that was later embodied in the project Columbia University Research in Contemporary Cultures. "Anthropology and the Humanities" (1948), her address as the retiring president of the American Anthropological Association, rounds out her professional life.

Certain parts of her writing are not represented. She wrote and lectured widely on race relations as well as on other contemporary subjects of controversy. She wrote many scholarly reviews. In addition, she reviewed a procession of rather miscellaneous books, published in *Books* (the *New York Herald Tribune*'s weekly book review), *The Nation*, *The New Republic*, and other magazines, an activity which provided money to be used for students' needs before she had other resources on which to draw for this purpose. Her poems, of which her own selection made in 1941 appears in *An Anthropologist at Work*, were all written early in her career; their inclusion would have somewhat distorted the sequence of work presented here. But the reader can always turn to *An Anthropologist at Work*, which is readily available and contains a much larger and broader selection of her writing.

The articles included here stand on their own merits. They do not, I believe, require further interpretation if they are read in the context provided by the biography.

Configurations of Culture in North America

✦ It is one of the philosophical justifications for the study of primitive peoples that ethnological data may make clear fundamental social facts that are otherwise confused and not open to demonstration. Of these none seem to me more important than this of fundamental and distinctive configurations in culture that so pattern existence and condition the emotional and cognitive reactions of its carriers that they become incommensurables, each specializing in certain selected types of behavior and each ruling out the behavior proper to its opposites.

REPRODUCED BY PERMISSION of the American Anthropological Association from *American Anthropologist* 34:1–27 (1932); abridged.

I have recently examined from this point of view two types of cultures represented in the Southwest,[1] that of the Pueblo contrasted with those of the various surrounding peoples. I have called the *ethos* of the Pueblo Apollonian in Nietzsche's sense of the cultural pursuit of sobriety, of measure, of the distrust of excess and orgy. On the other hand Nietzsche's contrasted type, the Dionysian, is abundantly illustrated in all the surrounding cultures. It values excess as escape to an order of existence beyond that of the five senses, and finds its expression in the creation in culture of painful and dangerous experiences, and in the cultivation of emotional and psychic excesses, in drunkenness, in dreams, and in trance.

The situation in the Southwest gives an exceptionally good opportunity for the study of the extent to which contrasted psychological sets of this sort, once they have become institutionalized, can shape the resulting cultures. The Pueblo are a clearly marked-off civilization of very considerable known antiquity, islanded in the midst of highly divergent cultures. But this islanding of their culture cannot be set down as in Oceania to the facts of the physical environment. There are no mountain ranges, no impassable deserts, not even many miles that separate them from their neighbors. It is a cultural islanding achieved almost in the face of geographical conditions. The eastern Pueblo went regularly to the plains for the buffalo hunt, and the center of the Pima country is within a day's run on foot of Hopi and Zuñi. The fact therefore that they have a complex culture set off as strikingly as any in North America from that of their impinging neighbors makes the situation unmistakable. The resistance that has kept out of the Pueblo [2] such traits as that of the guardian spirit and the vision, the shaman, the torture, the orgy, the cultural use of intoxicants, the ideas of mystic danger associated with sex, initiative of the individual and personal authority in social affairs, is a cultural resistance, not the result of an isolation due to physical facts of the environment.

The culture of the southwest Pueblo, as I have pointed out in the article referred to above, is a thoroughgoing, institutionalized elaboration of the theme of sobriety and restraint in behavior. This dominating theme has effectually prevented the development of those typical Dionysian situ-

[1] Psychological Types in the Cultures of the Southwest, in *Proceedings of the Twenty-third International Congress of Americanists, September 1928* (New York, 1930), pp. 572–81.
[2] *Ibid.*, pp. 573 ff.

ations which most North American tribes elaborate out of every phase of life, cultivating abandon and emotional excesses, and making birth, adolescence, menstruation, the dead, the taking of life, and any other life crises ambivalently charged occasions fraught with danger and with power. It has likewise refused such traits of surrounding cultures as self-torture, ceremonially used drugs, and the inspirational vision, along with all the authority that is usually derived from personal contact with the supernatural, i.e., shamanism. It hates disruptive impulses in the individual—I speak in an animistic shorthand, meaning that their cultural bias is opposed to and finally pares down to a minimum the potential human impulses to see visions and experiment in indulgences and work off its energy in excesses of the flesh.

Among these disruptive impulses the Pueblo *ethos* counts also the will to power. Just as surely as it has acted to obliterate self-torture it has acted to obliterate the human impulse toward the exercise of authority. Their ideal man avoids authority in the home or in public office. He has office at last thrust upon him, but even at that the culture has already taken away from the position he has to occupy anything that approaches personal authority in our sense; it remains a position of trust, a center of reference in planning the communal program, not much more.

Sanction for all acts comes always from the formal structure, not from the individual. He may not kill unless he has the power of the scalp or is planning to be initiated into it—that is, into the organized war society. He may not doctor because he knows how or acquires sanction from any personal encounter with the supernatural, but because he has bought his way up to the highest rank in the curing societies. Even if he is the chief priest he will not plant a prayer stick except at the institutionally prescribed seasons; if he does he will be regarded as practicing sorcery, as, according to the point of tales in which this situation occurs, he is indeed. The individual devotes himself therefore to the constituted forms of his society. He takes part in all cult activity, and according to his means will increase the number of masks possessed in Zuñi by having one made for himself—which involves feasting and considerable expense. He will undertake to sponsor the calendric kachina dances; he will entertain them at the great winter dance by building them a new house and assuming the expenses of his share of the ceremony. But he does all this with an anonymity that is hard to duplicate from other cultures. He does not undertake them as bids for personal prestige. Socially the good man never raises himself above his neighbor by displaying authority. He sets everyone at his ease, he "talks lots," he gives no occasion for offense. He is never violent, nor at the mercy of his emotions.

The whole interest of the culture is directed toward providing for every situation sets of rules and practices by means of which one gets by without resort to the violence and disruption that their culture distrusts. Even fertility practices, associated so universally in other cultures with excess and orgy, though they make them the leading motif of their religion,[3] are non-erotic rites based on analogies and sympathetic magic. I shall discuss later the thoroughness with which their rites of mourning are designed to this same end.

Such configurations of culture, built around certain selected human traits and working toward the obliteration of others are of first-rate importance in the understanding of culture. Traits objectively similar and genetically allied may be utilized in different configurations, it may be, without change in detail. The relevant facts are the emotional background against which the act takes place in the two cultures. It will illustrate this if we imagine the Pueblo snake dance in the setting of our own society. Among the western Pueblo, at least, repulsion is hardly felt for the snake. They have no physiological shudder at the touch of its body; in the ceremony, they are not flying in the face of a deep antipathy and horror. When we identify ourselves with them we are emotionally poles apart, though we put ourselves meticulously into the pattern of their behavior. For them, the poison of the rattlesnakes being removed, the whole procedure is upon the level of a dance with eagles or with kittens. It is a completely characteristic Apollonian dance expression, whereas with us, with our emotional reaction to the snake, the dance is not possible upon this level. Without changing an item of the outward behavior of the dance, its emotional significance and its functioning in the culture are reversed. And yet often enough, in ethnographic monographs, we are at a loss to know this emotional background even in traits where it becomes of first-rate importance, as for instance in the feeling directed toward the corpse.

[3] H. K. Haeberlin, The Idea of Fertilization in the Culture of the Pueblo Indians, *Memoirs of the American Anthropological Association*, No. 3 (1916).

We need much more relevant data from the field in order to evaluate the emotional background.

The more usual situation is the one in which the trait is reworked to express the different emotional patterning characteristic of the culture that has adopted it. This reworking of widespread behavior traits into different configurations of culture can only be adequately described when there is a much greater body of field data presented from this angle, and a much greater agreement has been arrived at among anthropologists as to the relevant patternings. There are however certain configurations of culture that are clear from the existing monographs, and not only, nor chiefly perhaps, from America. However in order to establish the validity of the argument I am presenting, I shall limit myself to traits diffused over this continent and discuss only well-known North American cultural traits and the way in which they have been shaped by the dominant drives of certain contrasted cultures.

I have already referred to death practices. There are two aspects involved in death practices which I shall consider separately: on the one hand, the bereavement situation, and on the other, the situation of the individual who has killed another.

The bereavement situation is characteristically handled in Dionysian and in Apollonian cultures according to their bias. Dionysian behavior for the bereaved has found several different channels of expression in the region we are discussing in North America. Among the western Plains it was a violent expression of loss and upheaval. Abandon took the form of self-mutilation, especially for women. They gashed their heads, their calves, they cut off fingers. Long lines of women marched through camp after the death of an important person, their legs bare and bleeding. The blood on their heads and legs they let cake and did not remove. When the body was taken out for burial everything in the lodge was thrown on the ground for any that were not relatives to possess themselves of it. The lodge was pulled down and given to another. Soon everything was gone and the widow had nothing left but the blanket about her. At the grave the man's favorite horses were killed and both men and women wailed for the dead. A wife or daughter might remain at the grave, wailing and refusing to eat, for twenty-four hours, until her relatives dragged her

away. At intervals, even twenty years after a death had occurred, on passing the grave they cried for the dead.[4]

On the death of children especially, abandon of grief is described as
being indulged. Suicide is often resorted to by one parent or the other.
According to Denig, among the Assiniboine:

*should anyone offend the parent during this time his death would most
certainly follow, as the man, being in profound sorrow, seeks something
on which to wreak his revenge, and he soon after goes to war, to kill or
be killed, either being immaterial to him in that state.*[5]

Such descriptions are characteristic of Plains mourning. They have in
common fundamental social patternings of violent and uninhibited grief.
This has nothing to do, of course, with the question of whether this is the
emotion called up in all those who participate in the rites; the point at
issue is only that in this region institutionalized behavior at this crisis is
patterned upon free emotional indulgence.

In such a typical Apollonian culture as the pueblo of Isleta, on the
other hand, Plains mourning is unthinkable. Isleta, like any other Apollonian society provides itself with rules by which to outlaw violence and
aggressive moods of any kind. Strong feeling is repulsive to it and even at
death, which is the most stubbornly unescapable of the tragic occasions
of life, their whole emphasis is to provide a routine for getting by with the
least possible upheaval. In Isleta a priest who is known as the Black Corn
Mother and who is a functionary of one of the four "Corn" divisions of
the Pueblo, officiates at death. He is called immediately and prepares the
corpse, brushing the hair and washing and painting the face with identification marks to indicate the social affiliation of the dead. After this the
relatives come in, bringing each a candle to the dead, and the Corn
Mother prays and sends the people away again. When they have gone he
and his helpers "feed" the dead man ceremonially with the left hand—as-

[4] George Bird Grinnell, *The Cheyenne Indians*, 2 vols. (New Haven: Yale University Press, 1923), 2:162.
[5] Edwin T. Denig, The Assiniboine, *Forty-sixth Annual Report of the Bureau of American Ethnology* (Washington, 1930), p. 573.

sociated with ghosts—and make an altar in the room. Only once again during all this ritual tending of the dead are the relatives admitted, and that is when the priest has ready a small smudge from the combings of the dead man's hair. The bereaved breathe this in and will thereby cease to grieve over the dead person. The burial takes place the following day, but the family and relatives are ceremonially taboo for four days and remain in retreat in the house of the dead man, receiving certain ritual washings from the priest. The formalities that more nearly correspond to burial in other regions are performed over the burial of food for the deceased on the fourth day. They go outside the village for this, and after it is over, they break the pot in which water was carried, and the hair-brush that was used to prepare the body for burial, and on their return cut their trail with a deep incision with a flint knife. They listen and hear the dead man come, far off, to the place where they buried food for him. The house is filled with people awaiting their return, and the Black Corn Mother preaches to them, telling them this is the last time they need be afraid of the dead man's returning. The four days has been as four years to him and therefore those who remain will be the readier to forget. The relatives go to their houses but the housemates observe the or-dinary taboos for ceremonial purity for eight days more, after which ev-erything is over. The Black Corn Mother goes to the cacique and returns to him the power he received from him and must always receive from him for every death, but which he has this means of disposing of when he is not compelled to exercise it. It is a characteristic Apollonian touch, and very common in the Southwest.[6]

There is here no frank institutionalized indulgence in grief, no cutting off of fingers—not even of hair—no gashing of bodies, no destruction of property, not even a show of its distribution. Instead of insistence upon prolonged mourning by the most closely bereaved, the emphasis is all upon immediate forgetting. The two pictures are of course familiar types of contrasted behavior, and they are here institutionalized for two con-trasted cultures.

In the face of the evident opposition of these two institutionalized types of behavior it is at first sight somewhat bizarre to group them together

---

[6] Esther Schiff Goldfrank, Isleta ms.

over against another type in contrast to which they are at one. It is true nevertheless. In their different contexts, the Southwest and the Plains are alike in not capitalizing ideas of pollution and dread. This is not to say that fear of contamination or of the dangerous power of the dead are never to be detected in these regions; they are humanly potential attitudes and no culture is perhaps hermetically sealed against them. But the culture does not capitalize them. In contrast with the non-Pueblo Southwest, for instance, these two are alike in realistically directing their behavior toward the loss-situation instead of romantically elaborating the danger situation. In Isleta the clan head officiating at death does not have to be purified and the curse of contact with the dead lifted from him when the rites are over; he lays aside his official prerogatives as undertaker as he would his stole. He has not been polluted by his office. Nor is the smudge for the relatives designed to put them beyond the pursuit of vengefulness of the dead, but rather to make them forget quickly.[7] They break his hairbrush, not the bones of his legs, because what they are symbolizing is the ending of this man's life not precautions against his envy and vindictiveness. Similarly on the Plains [8] the giving away of property and the demeaning of one's self in personal appearance, which is so commonly a ruse for forestalling the jealousy of the deceased, is here a gesture of grief and associated with such other manifestations of oblivion of one's self and ordinary routine as going off mourning alone on the prairies, or starting off "to kill or be killed, either being immaterial to him" in his grief. They do not destroy the tipi and all the man's horses, for they are neither concerned with the contamination of the corpse nor with the malice of the ghost toward those who continue to enjoy them. On the contrary their one thought is to give them away. Neither do they capitalize that common theme for patterning a danger situation, the fear and hatred of the person who has used supernatural power to kill the deceased.

These themes however are the very basis of the mourning ceremony in surrounding regions. It is no uncommon thing to find that death rites are hardly directed at all toward the loss-situation but wholly preoccupied

[7] In Zuni however certain scalp dance attitudes are explicitly associated with the widow and widower.
[8] In this entire discussion I exclude the Southern Sioux.

with contamination. The Navaho are by no means extreme examples. The Franciscan Fathers [9] tell us that in former times slaves were employed to prepare and carry the corpse and they were killed at the grave. Now members of the family must expose themselves to this defilement. Men and women strip themselves to a breechcloth for the duty and leave the hair flowing so that not even a hair string may be exposed. To the Navaho either type of behavior we have just been describing would be unthinkable. Only those who because of their close kinship cannot avoid the duty accompany the body. Four are necessary, one to lead the favorite horse which is to be killed on the grave of his master, two to carry the corpse, and one to warn any travelers along the way that they may turn aside and save themselves from defilement. To protect themselves the mourners keep strict silence. Meantime the hogan in which death occurred has been burnt to the ground. All the members of the family fast for four days and during this time a guard warns all comers off the trail between the hogan and the grave lest they incur danger.[10]

Besides the dominating fear of pollution, the Navaho have a strong fear also of the return of the ghost. If a woman fails in fasting or breaks silence, it will show the dead the way back and the ghost will harm the offender. This discomfort of the living before the dead is nearly universal, though it assumes very different proportions in different cultures.

On the other hand, the dreaded vengefulness of the ghost and his malice toward those who have been spared by death is not as popular in North America in the elaboration of the horror situation as it is in South America and in other parts of the world. It is a theme that for Crawley, for example, is fundamental in death practices, and it is striking that it should play so slight a role in North America. One of the clearest examples on this continent is from the Fox. The Central Algonkin have a strong belief in cruel antagonists which the dead must overcome along their route, and the custom of burying weapons with the body was in order that they might be armed against them. With the Winnebago, too,[11] war hatchets were buried with the dead so that they might kill

---

[9] *An Ethnologic Dictionary of the Navajo Language* (St. Michael's Arizona, 1910), p. 454.
[10] Gladys A. Reichard, *Social Life of the Navajo Indians* (New York: Columbia University Press, 1928), p. 142.
[11] Paul Radin, Winnebago Tales, *Journal of American Folk-Lore* 22:312 (1909).

animals they met along their way, and their relatives in this world be blessed in like fashion. But Jones records that among the Fox it was a frequent request of the dying that they might be provided in the grave with a war hatchet to protect themselves against Cracker of Skulls; but this the living would not do because the dead were feared and it was desirable that they be weaponless. Therefore they are helpless before Cracker of Skulls who scoops from each a fingerful of brain. [12]

The Mohave on the other hand made much of the fear and blame of the medicine-man who had supernaturally caused the death. A seer was employed to visit the land of the dead after a death. If the deceased was not there, it was known that the doctor who attended him was guilty of malpractice. "It is the nature of these doctors to kill people in this way just as it is the nature of hawks to kill little birds for a living," according to a Mohave in the 80's. A rich man remained rich in the other world and all those a medicine-man killed were under his chieftainship. He desired a large rich band. "I've killed only two. When I die I want to rule a bigger band than that." [13] When blame was attached to any medicine-man, anyone might take it upon himself to kill him.

The medicine-man openly avowed his complicity. He might hand a stick to a man and say, "I killed your father." Or he might come and tell a sick person, "Don't you know that it is I that am killing you? Must I grasp you and despatch you with my hands before you will try to kill me?" [14] The point is that this is supernatural killing. There has never been any intimation that it was the custom for a medicine-man to use poison or knife. It is a blame- and terror-situation open and declared, a situation more familiar in Africa than in North America.

It is well to contrast this Mohave attitude with the Pueblo witchcraft theories. In Zuñi the bereavement situation is not lost in a situation of sorcery and of vengeance taken upon sorcery; bereavement is handled as bereavement, however clearly the emphasis is upon putting it by as soon as possible. In spite of the great amount of anxiety about witches which is

[12] William Jones, Mortuary Observances and the Adoption Rites of the Algonkin Foxes of Iowa, in *Quinzième Congrès International des Américanistes* (Quebec, 1906), pp. 263–78.
[13] John J. Bourke, Notes on the Cosmology and Theogony of the Mojave Indians of the Rio Grande, Arizona, *Journal of American Folk-Lore* 2:175 (1889).
[14] A. L. Kroeber, Handbook of the Indians of California, *Bureau of American Ethnology Bulletin* No. 78 (Washington, 1925), p. 778.

always present among the Pueblo, at an actual death little attention is paid to the possibility of their complicity. Only in an epidemic when death becomes a public menace is the witch theory ordinarily acted upon. And it is a community anxiety neurosis, not a Dionysian situation depending like the Mohave on the exercise of the shaman's will to supernatural power, and the ambivalent attitude of the group toward this power. I doubt whether anyone in Zuñi has any witch techniques which he actually practices; no one defies another over a dead or dying man. It is never the medicine-man who by virtue of his medicine powers is also the death bringer and embodies in his one person the characteristic Dionysian double aspects of power. Death is not dramatized as a duel between a shaman, thought of as a bird of prey, and his victim. Even the existence of all the necessary ideas among the Pueblo—it is interesting that they are overwhelmingly European in their detail—does not lead to this Dionysian interpretation of death.

There are other themes upon which danger situations can be and have been built up around death in different cultures. The point we need for our discussion is that the Dionysian indulgence in emotion at death can be institutionalized around realistic grief at the loss of a member of the community, or around various constructs such as contamination, guilt, and the vengefulness of the dead. The contrast between cultures which indulge in danger constructs of this sort in every situation in life and those that do not is as striking as that between the Apollonian-Dionysian types.

The fullest collections of primitive material on the danger situation are of course the various works of Crawley. This was his outstanding subject throughout his work, and he interpreted it as a universal drive in human society. It is certainly one that is common in institutional behavior, but it is for all its wide distribution a particular configuration of culture, and contrasting configurations develop their contrasting behaviors.

Where human contacts, the crises of life, and a wide range of acts are regarded realistically in any culture, and especially without the metamorphosis that passes over them in consequence of the fear- and contamination-constructs we have been discussing, and this is institutionalized in culture, I shall call them realists. Cultures of the opposite type I shall call simply non-realists. It is admittedly poor terminology. James's antithesis of the tough and tender-minded approaches also the distinction I wish to make, but his substitute for these of healthy-mindedness and the sick soul brings in an implication I wish to avoid.

We must be content to say, I think, that those cultures that institutionalize death as loss, adolescence as an individual's growing up, mating as sex choice, killing as success in a fight, and so on, contrast strongly with those who live in an Aladdin's cave where all the vegetation is something else. It is certainly one of the most striking facts of anthropology that primary life situations are so seldom read off culturally in this direct and realistic fashion.

Indeed it is the realistic institutions that would seem to be the less thoroughly carried through. Human culture as a whole throughout its history has been based on certain non-realistic notions, of which animism and incest are the ones which will occur to every anthropologist. The fear of the ghost—not of his enmity or vengefulness, which is found only locally, but of his mere wraith—is another. These notions appear to have conditioned the human race from the beginning, and it is obviously impossible to go back to their beginnings or discuss the attitudes that gave them birth. For the purposes of this discussion we must accept them as we have to accept the fact that we have five fingers. Even the realistic Plains have not discarded them, though they use them more realistically than other cultures.

In the region we are discussing, the Dionysian cultures are cross-sectioned by this realist-nonrealist antithesis, the Plains institutionalizing excess and abandon without elaborating danger-situations, and the non-Pueblo Southwest, the Shoshoneans, and the Northwest Coast carrying these danger-situations to extremes. The realist cultures likewise are Dionysian among the Plains and Apollonian among the Pueblo. The two categories operate at a different level and cross-section each other. It is difficult, however, to imagine an Apollonian culture maintaining itself on the basis of fundamental danger-constructs, and certainly this type does not occur in the region we are considering.

It is impossible to do justice here to the consistency of this realist configuration among the western Plains; it would be necessary first to differentiate their institutional behavior from the Apollonian Pueblo and then from the romantics about them. So far as the people directly to the west, the Shoshoneans, are concerned, the differences in behavior which I wish to stress have already been pointed out by Lowie.[15] He notices the change in affect in menstrual taboos [16] and the dropping out of the relevant customs. Childbirth and the menstruating woman have been two of the great points of departure for the tender-minded elaboration of horror and the uncanny. The Plains, like the Pueblo, do not share the trait. Lowie points out also how the Plains, again like the Pueblo, stand contrasted with the western groups in ignoring the non-realistic involvement of the husband in his wife's confinement. Attenuated forms of couvade are the rule for Shoshoneans, Plateau peoples, and Californians. It is not a Plains trait.

The same disinclination is evident in the contrasting attitude toward the name.[17] Plains names are not mystic part and parcel of one's personality; they are realistic appellations much in our own sense. It is not a grievous insult to ask another's name. Even more, it is not an affair of life and death to use the name of another after his death. Among the Karok,[18] for instance, the same retribution must be visited upon this act as upon having taken the man's life. It is a fiction that is alien on the Plains.

There are therefore a considerable number of reasons for thinking that the cultural attitude we have noted in Plains mourning ceremonies over against those to the west and south (Navaho and Pima) are characteristic for their culture. Most striking of all perhaps, Lowie points out that among the western Plains vengeance upon the medicine man is atypical whereas it is reported among the Shoshoneans and the central Californians. I believe this can be put very much more strongly. In any other part of the world than North America we should frankly refer to the attitude that is constantly reported from British Columbia to the Pima as sorcery, and the killing of the shaman as vengeance taken on the sorcerer. The Plains simply do not make anything of this pattern. They use super-

[15] Robert H. Lowie, The Cultural Connection of California and Plateau Shoshonean Tribes, *California University Publications in American Archaeology and Ethnology* 20:145–56 (1923).

[16] *Ibid.*, p. 145.

[17] *Ibid.*, p. 149.

[18] Stephen Powers, Tribes of California, *Contributions to North American Ethnology* 3:33 (1877).

natural power to further their own exploits as warriors, they do not use it to build up threats. Sorcery is the prime institutionalization of the neurotic's fear world, and it does not find place from the Blackfoot to the Cheyenne.

Before we continue with further examples of mourning practices in other configurations, it will be clearer to illustrate the configurations we have just discussed by another situation—the situation of the man who has killed another. It throws into relief the attitudes we have been discussing.

The Cheyenne scalp dance is characteristic of Plains configuration. Tremendous Dionysian exaltation is achieved, but not by way of horror or contamination ideas connected with the corpse; it is an uninhibited triumph, a gloating over the enemy who has been put out of the way. There is no intimation of a curse lying upon the scalper which it is the function of the dance to remove. There is no idea of the fearful potency of the scalp. It is a completely joyous occasion, a celebration of triumph and the answer to a prayer that had been made with tears.

Before setting out upon a warpath everything is solemn and prayerful, even sorrowful, in order to gain pity from the supernaturals.[19] On the return with the scalps, however, all is changed. The party falls upon the home camp by surprise at daybreak, the favorite hour for Indian attack, their faces blackened in triumph

> . . . *shooting off their guns and waving the poles on which were the scalps that had been taken. The people were excited and welcomed them with shouts and yells. All was joy. The women sang songs of victory. . . . In the front rank were those who had . . . counted coups. . . . Some threw their arms around the successful warriors. Old men and women sang songs in which the names were mentioned. The relatives of those who rode in the first rank . . . testified to their joy by making gifts to friends or to poor people. The whole crowd might go to where some brave man lived or to where his father lived, and there dance in his honor. They were likely to prepare to dance all night, and perhaps to keep up this dancing for two days and two nights.*[20]

[19] *Ibid.*, p. 22
[20] Grinnell, *Cheyenne Indians* 2:6–22.

Grinnell speaks especially of the fact that there was no ceremonial recognition of the priest or of his services on their return. The scalp was an emblem of victory and something to rejoice over. If members of the war party had been killed the scalps were thrown away and there was no scalp dance. But if the warrior who had been killed had counted coup before he died there was no occasion for grief, so great was the honor, and the victory celebration over the scalp went forward.

Everyone joined in the scalp dance. In keeping with its social character it was in charge of berdaches who were here matchmakers and "good company" and who took the place of the female relative who usually has so conspicuous a role. They called out the dances and carried the scalps. Old men and women came out as clowns, and as if anything were wanting to emphasize the absence among the Cheyenne of dread and danger in relation to the slain enemy, Grinnell says that some of these were dressed to represent the very warriors whose scalps were the center of the ceremony.[21]

This Plains behavior was unthinkable over a great part of the continent. In the southern belt of the United States, from the Natchez to the Mohave—excluding the Pueblo for the moment—the opposite attitude is at its height. Over this whole area the point of the scalp dance was the great dangerous supernatural potency of the scalp and the curse that must be removed from the slayer. It belonged to their whole tender-minded awe before dark and uncanny forces.

Years ago in the government warfare against the Apache the inexorable purification ceremonies of the Pima almost canceled their usefulness to the United States troops as allies. Their loyalty and bravery were undoubted, but upon the killing of an enemy each slayer must retire for twenty days of ceremonial purification. He selected a ceremonial father who cared for him and performed the rites. This father had himself taken life and been through the purification ceremonies. He sequestered the slayer in the bush in a small pit where he remained fasting for sixteen days, each four days with a plunge into the river, no matter what the weather, and a slight change in the rules of fasting. Among the Papago the father feeds him on the end of a long pole.[22] His wife must observe

[21] *Ibid.*, pp. 39–44.
[22] D. D. Gaillard, The Papago of Arizona and Sonora, *American Anthropologist* 7:293–96 (1894).

similar taboos in her own house. On the sixteenth day the dance occurs. The slayer sits again in a small pit in the middle of the dance circle, a hole that allows him only the most cramped position, and the "braves," men who have qualified as warriors, dance for him. The end of the Papago ceremony is the rite of throwing the slayer, bound hand and foot, into the river, after which he is loosed from his bonds, physically and spiritually. A bit of the hair of the man he has killed is placed by his "father" in a buckskin bag along with an owl feather to insure its blindness and a hawk feather to kill it, and by the ceremony this medicine is made subservient to his will. He embraces it, calling it "child," and uses it thereafter to bring rain.[23] The whole ceremony is one for drawing the teeth of a dangerous power and freeing the perpetrator from curse, to the end that the power may be rendered beneficent.

The Mohave had a ceremony of which we have less detail. The master of ceremonies alone could touch the scalp during the four-day ceremonies and he had to incense himself eight times daily.[24]

As I pointed out in a previous discussion of the Southwest, there is no culture trait in Zuñi that presents so many unmodified likenesses to institutions outside the Pueblo as the scalp dance. From the point of view of Pueblo cultural attitudes it presents strikingly atypical elements which are well-known for the central region of North America and at home there. One such is the biting of the scalp, reported from Laguna [25] and Zuñi. This act is performed in the face of a strong feeling of contamination from the scalp. In Zuñi they say that the woman upon whom this act devolves is free of the curse because she rises to the point of "acting like an animal." It is an almost unique recognition in this culture of the state of ecstasy, and is an instance of a diffused culture trait, the scalp dance, which has been accepted among the Pueblo without the reconstruction that would have been necessary to bring it into line with their dominant attitudes.

Accepting this fact, we may examine the Zuñi scalp dance to see in

[23] Frank Russell, The Pima Indians, *Twenty-sixth Annual Report of the Bureau of American Ethnology* (Washington, 1908), p. 204; J. William Lloyd, *Aw-aw-Tam Indian Nights* (Westfield, N.J., 1911), p. 90; and Ruth Benedict, MS.

[24] Kroeber, Handbook, p. 572.

[25] Franz Boas, Keresan Texts, *Publications of the American Ethnological Society* 8:290 (1928).

what directions it has been modified at their hands. In the first place, they have rephrased the release from the curse so that it is no longer, as with the Pima and Papago, a dramatization of ambivalent attitudes toward the sacred—on the one hand, the polluting, on the other, the powerful—but belongs with any retreat undertaken to gain membership in a society. The scalp dance in Zuñi is an initiation into the policing society of the bow priesthood. It is taken up into their pattern of providing formal fraternal organizations for handling every situation. The bow priesthood is an elaborate organization with special responsibilities, functioning for life. The curse of the slayer and the release from it are dwarfed by the pattern of initiation into a new set of social functions.

Similarly the cleaning of the scalp, which in more Dionysian cultures is done with the tongue, lapping the fresh drops of blood, in Zuñi is an adoption rite, a baptism in clear water which is performed by the father's sisters to give status in the clan group. It must be performed not only at adoption but at marriage, and, as we have seen, in the scalp ceremony. The idea underlying the act in Zuñi is that of adoption of a new, beneficent influence into tribal status—surely a clear example of the way in which Pueblo configurations draw the teeth of more violent behaviors.

Their attitude is especially clear in the scalp dance prayers:

For indeed the enemy
Even though on rubbish
He lived and grew to maturity
By virtue of the corn priests' rain prayers
(He has become valuable.)
Indeed the enemy
Though in his life
He was a person given to falsehood
He has become one to foretell
How the world will be,
How the days will be . . .
Even though he was without value,
Yet he was a water being,
He was a seed being,
Desiring the enemy's waters,

Desiring his seeds,
Desiring his wealth,
Eagerly you shall await his days (the scalp dance).
When with your clear water
You have bathed the enemy (the scalp),
When in the corn priests' water-filled court
He has been set up,
All the corn priest's children
With the song sequences of the fathers
Will be dancing for him.
And whenever all his days are past,
Then a good day,
A beautiful day,
A day filled with great shouting,
With great laughter,
A good day,
With us, your children,
You will pass.[26]

It is not dread and horror that find expression in such lines as these. In-stead the attention is realistically turned upon his unremarkable mortal existence, and the contrast is made with his present beneficence as a means toward rain and crops.

Both the bereavement situation and the murder situation show there-fore strong contrasts in the three North American cultural configurations we have considered. I shall arbitrarily select one other contrasting config-uration that is perhaps nowhere in the world more strikingly illustrated than in North America. The pursuit of personal aggrandizement on the Northwest Coast is carried out in such a way that it approaches an institu-tionalization of the megalomaniac personality type. The censorship which is insisted upon in civilizations like our own is absent in such self-glorifications as a Kwakiutl public address, and when censorship func-tions, as among the tribes of the gulf of Georgia, their self-abasements are

[26] Ruth Bunzel, Zuni Ritual Poetry, *Forty-seventh Annual Report of the Bureau of Ameri-can Ethnology* (Washington, 1932), pp. 611–835.

patently not expressions of humility but equivalents of the familiar self-glorification of the Kwakiutl. Any of their songs illustrate the usual tenor:

I am the great chief who makes people ashamed.
I am the great chief who makes people ashamed.
Our chief brings shame to the faces.
Our chief brings jealousy to the faces.
Our chief makes people cover their faces by what he is continually doing
   in this world
Giving again and again oil feasts to all the tribes.[27]

. . . .

I began at the upper end of the tribes. Serves them right! Serves them
   right!
I came downstream setting fire to the tribes with my fire-bringer.
Serves them right! Serves them right!
My name, just my name, killed them, I, the great Mover of the world.
   Serves them right! Serves them right![28]

The energy of the culture is frankly given to competition in a game of raising one's personal status and of entrenching oneself by the humiliation of one's fellows. In a lesser degree this pursuit of personal prestige is characteristic of the Plains. But the picture is sharply contrasted. The Plains do not institutionalize the inferiority complex and its compensations. They do not preoccupy themselves with the discovery of insults in every situation. They are anything but paranoid. But it is in terms of these particular psychological sets that the pursuit of personal aggrandizement is carried out in the culture of the North Pacific coast. Probably the inferiority complex has never been so blatantly institutionalized. The greatest range of acts are regarded as insults, not only personal derogatory acts, but all untoward events like a cut from an axe or the overturning of a canoe. All such events threaten the ego security of the members of this paranoid-like civilization, and according to their pattern may be wiped out by the distribution of property. If they cannot be, the response is per-

[27] Franz Boas, Ethnology of the Kwakiutl, *Thirty-fifth Annual Report of the Bureau of American Ethnology* (Washington, 1921), p. 1291.
[28] *Ibid.*, p. 1381.

fectly in character: the bubble of self-esteem is pricked and the man re-
tires to his pallet for weeks at a time, or, it may be, takes his life. This extreme of negative self-feeling is far removed from the exhibitions of
shame due to indecent exposures or breaking of taboo in other regions. It
is plain sulking, the behavior of a person whose self-esteem is all he has
and who has been wounded in his pride.

All the circumstances of life are regarded on the Northwest Coast, not
as occasions for violent grief or equally violent jubilation, occasions for
freely expending energy in differentiated ways, but primarily as further-
ing, all of them alike, this insult contest. They are occasions for the
required fight for prestige. Sex, the life cycle, death, warfare, are all almost equivalent raw material for cultural patterning to this end. A girl's
adolescence is an event for which her father gathers property for ten years
in order to demonstrate his greatness by a great distribution of wealth; it is
not as a fact in the girl's sex life that it figures in their culture, but as a
rung of her father's ladder toward higher social standing, therefore also of
her own. For since in this region all property that is distributed must be
paid back with usury (else the recipient will entirely lose face), to make
oneself poor is the prime act in acquiring wealth. Even a quarrel with
one's wife is something only a great man may indulge in, for it entails
the distribution of all his property, even to the rafters of his house. But
if the chief has enough wealth for this distribution of property, he wel-
comes the occasion as he does his daughter's puberty as a rung in the
ladder of advancement.[29]

This comes out clearly in the reinterpretation of the bereavement situation in this region. Even the cutting of the hair in mourning has become
not an act of grief on the part of near relatives, but the service of the opposite phratry signifying their tribute to the greatness of the deceased, and
the fact that the relatives of the dead are able to recompense them.
Similarly it also is another step upward in the pursuit of prestige and the
acquisition of wealth. All the services for the dead are carried out in like
manner. The emphasis of the society at death fell upon the distribution
of property by the bereaved phratry to the officiating opposite phratry.
Without reference to its character as a loss- or danger-situation, it was

[29] *Ibid.*, p. 1359.

used just as the occasion of the girl's first menstruation or a domestic quarrel to demonstrate the solvency of the family group and to put down rival claimants to like wealth. Among the Haida [30] the great funeral potlatch, a year after the death, where this property was distributed, was organized around the transfer of winter-dance society membership to members of the host's phratry from members of the guests' phratry, in return for the property that was being distributed to them—an activity of course that has reference to ideas of ownership and prestige and winter ceremonial among the Haida but not to the loss involved in death nor yet to the danger associated with the corpse or the ghost. As the Kwakiutl say "they fight with property"—i.e., to achieve and maintain status based on wealth and inherited prerogatives; therefore "they fight," also, with a funeral.

This reinterpretation of the bereavement situation in terms of the "fight with property" is, however, only a part of the Northwest Coast pattern of behavior. It is assimilated as well to the insult preoccupation. The death of a relative, not only in a war but by sickness or accident, was an affront to be wiped out by the death of a person of another tribe. One was shamed until the score had been settled. The bereaved was dangerous in the way any man was who had been grievously shamed. When the chief Neqapenkem's sister and her daughter did not come back from Victoria either, people said, because their boat capsized or they drank bad whiskey, he called together the warriors. "Now I ask you tribes, who shall wail? Shall I do it or shall another?" The foremost responded, "Not you, Chief, let some other of the tribes." They set up the war pole, and the others came forward saying, "We came here to ask you to go to war that someone else may wail on account of our deceased sister." So they started out with full war rites to "pull under" the Sanetch for the chief's dead relatives. They found seven men and two children asleep and killed all except one girl whom they took captive. [31]

Again, the chief Qaselas' son died, and he and his brother and uncle

---

[30] John R. Swanton, Contributions to the Ethnology of the Haida, in Franz Boas, ed., *The Jesup North Pacific Expedition*, 5, *Memoirs of The American Museum of Natural History*, 8 (New York, 1905–1909), pp. 176, 179.

[31] Boas, Ethnology of the Kwakiutl, p. 1363.

set out to wipe out the stain. They were entertained by Nengemalis at their first stop. After they had eaten, "Now I will tell you the news, Chief," Qaselas said. "My prince died today and you will go with him." So they killed their host and his wife. "Then Qaselas and his crew felt good when they arrived at Sebaa in the evening. . . . It is not called war, but 'to die with those that are dead.' " [32]

This is pure head hunting, a paranoid reading of bereavement that stands almost alone in North America. Here death is institutionalized in such practices as this as the major instance of the countless untoward events of life which confound a man's pride and are treated as insults. [33]

Both the preoccupation with prestige and the preoccupation with insults underlie also the behavior centered around the killing of an enemy. The victory dance has become permanent, graded societies institutionalizing the most fiercely guarded prerogatives of these tribes; they constitute one of the most elaborate prestige organizations we know anything about. The original trait upon which they were built is preserved among the tribes to the south. It was a victory dance with the head of the enemy held in the teeth. As Professor Boas has shown, this became, as it was worked up into the Northwest Coast configuration, the cannibal dance [34] and the pattern of the secret societies. The dancers of the Kwakiutl secret societies are still considered "warriors," and the societies, which are normally in operation only during the winter season, always function on a war party no matter what the season. Now these secret societies are the great validations of prestige and of wealth through the distribution of property, and the final Northwest Coast form of the germinal idea of the victory dance is therefore that of enormously elaborate,

---

[32] *Ibid.*, p. 1385.

[33] In this short survey I have emphasized the differentiated aspect of mourning on the Northwest Coast and omitted the strong institutionalization of death as uncleanliness in this region, as this trait is common to regions we have discussed. No area has carried further the idea of uncleanliness—mourners, menstruating women, women in childbirth, men and women after intercourse, are all unclean. This is institutionalized differently in different tribes as it comes into conflict with the prestige mechanisms.

[34] Franz Boas and Livingston Farrand, *The North-Western Tribes of Canada*, Twelfth and Final Report of the Sixty-eighth Meeting of the British Association for the Advancement of Science, 1898 (London: Murray, 1899).

rigidly prescribed secret societies, membership in which establishes and validates social status.[35]

The dominant drive being the competition for prerogatives, another turn is given to the situation of the person who has killed another. One can get prerogatives, according to their idea, not only through the death of relatives, but through that of a victim, so that if a person has been killed at my hands I may claim his prerogatives. The slayer's situation is therefore not one of circumventing a dread curse or of celebrating a triumph of personal prowess; it is one of distributing large amounts of wealth to validate the privileges he has taken by violence at the moment when, incidentally so far as institutional behavior goes, he took also the life of the owner. That is, the taking of life is dwarfed behind the immense edifice of behavior proper to the Northwest Coast configuration.

As in the bereavement situation, the pattern has led to the institutionalization of head hunting with all its rigid rules of procedure. Meled had killed the chief of the local group Gexsem.

If he (Meled) had paid a copper or if he had given his daughter to marry the elder brother of the one he had shot, then his local group would have been disgraced, because he paid in order not to be killed in return. Only those pay who are weak minded.

He did not pay, and he was killed in revenge. But the man who killed him on sight was not a member of the local group of the chief whose death he was avenging. That chief's mother paid the avenger a slave but it was a disgrace to her local group and in spite of Meled's death it was not counted that the stain upon the name of the dead chief's local group had been wiped out.

[35] It is obvious from the nature of the case that this Northwest Coast game of prestige can only be played by selected members of the community. A large proportion of the tribe is no more than audience to these principal players, and the configuration of life for them necessarily differs. We need particularly to understand these "fan" cultures and the psychological attitudes characteristic on the one hand of the actors and on the other of those who make up the audience.

If another man of the local group Gexsem had killed Meled, then there would have been no disgrace to their group and all the men would have stopped talking about it. [36]

Death on the North Pacific Coast, therefore, was primarily an insult situation and an occasion for the validation of prerogatives. It is taken up into the characteristic configuration of this region and made to serve the drives that were dominant in their culture.

There are of course aspects of culture, especially of material culture, which are independent of many of the aims and virtues a society may make for itself. I do not mean to imply that the fortunes of the sinew-backed bow will depend upon whether the culture is Dionysian or Apollonian. But the range of applicability of the point I am making is nevertheless greater than is generally supposed. Radin has for instance argued very cogently from Winnebago material for the great importance of individuality and individual initiative "among primitives." [37] Now the Plains and the Winnebago are among our great primitive examples, according to all observers, of high cultural evaluation of the individual. He is allowed institutionally guaranteed initiative in his life such as one cannot easily duplicate from other regions. One has only to compare it with the Pueblo to realize that Radin's point of very great personal initiative is a prime fact among the Winnebago and the western Plains, but not coextensive with primitive culture. It is an attitude to be studied independently in each area.

All this has a most important bearing on the formation and functioning of culture traits. We are too much in the habit of studying religion, let us say, or property complexes, as if the fundamental fact about them were dependable human response: like awe, for example, or the "acquisitive instinct," from which they stemmed. Now there have been human institutions that do show this direct correspondence to simple human emo-

---

[36] Boas, Ethnology of the Kwakiutl, p. 1360.
[37] Paul Radin, *Primitive Man as Philosopher* (New York: Appleton, 1927), pp. 32 ff.

tions—death practices that express grief, mating customs that express sex preference, agricultural practices that begin and end with the provisioning of the tribe. But even to list them in this fashion makes forcibly clear how difficult it is to find such examples. As a matter of fact, agriculture and economic life in general usually sets itself other ends than the satisfaction of the food quest, marriage usually expresses other things more strikingly than sex preference, and mourning notoriously does not stress grief. The more intimately we know the inner workings of different cultures the more readily we can see that the almost infinite variability in any cultural trait if it is followed around the globe is not a mere ringing of the changes upon some simple underlying human response. Another and greater force has been at work that has used the recurring situations of mating, death, provisioning, and the rest almost as raw material and elaborated them to express its own intent. This force that bends occasions to its purposes and fashions them to its own idiom we can call within that society its dominant drive. Some societies have brought all this raw material into conspicuous harmony with this dominant drive, the societies to which on an a priori basis Sapir would allow the appellation of "genuine cultures." [38] Many have not. Sapir holds that an honest self-consistency that rules out hypocritical pretensions is the mark of a genuine culture. It seems to me that cultures may be built solidly and harmoniously upon fantasies, fear-constructs, or inferiority complexes and indulge to the limit in hypocrisy and pretensions. The person who has an ineradicable drive to face the facts and avoid hypocrisy may be the outlaw of a culture that is nevertheless on its own basis symmetrical and harmonious. Because a configuration is well-defined it is not therefore honest.

It is, however, the reality of such configurations that is in question. I do not see that the development of these configurations in different societies is more mystic or difficult to understand than, for example, the development of an art style. In both if we have the available material we can see the gradual integration of elements, and growing dominance of some few stylistic drives. In both, also if we had the material, we could without doubt trace the influence of gifted individuals who have bent the culture in the direction of their own capacities. But the configuration of the cul-

[38] Edward Sapir, "Culture, Genuine and Spurious," *American Journal of Sociology* 29: 401–29 (1924).

ture nevertheless always transcends the individual elements that have gone to its making. The cultural configuration builds itself up over generations, discarding, as no individual may, the traits that are uncongenial to it. It takes to itself ritual and artistic and activational modes of expression that solidify its attitude and make it explicit. Many cultures have never achieved this thoroughgoing harmony. There are peoples who seem to shift back and forth between different types of behavior. Like our own civilization they may have received too many contradictory influences from different outside sources and been unable to reduce them to a common denominator. But the fact that certain people have not done so, no more makes it unnecessary to study culture from this angle than the fact that some languages shift back and forth between different fundamental grammatical devices in forming the plural or in designating tense, makes it unnecessary to study grammatical forms.

These dominant drives are as characteristic for individual areas as are house forms or the regulations of inheritance. We are too handicapped yet by lack of relevant descriptions of culture to know whether these drive-distributions are often coextensive with distribution of material culture, or whether in some regions there are many such to one culture area defined from more objective traits. Descriptions of culture from this point of view must include much that older field work ignored, and without the relevant field work all our propositions are pure romancing.

Magic

�֍ The basic ideas that have everywhere underlain magic have been limited. The practice of setting a pattern for the desired event, most frequently by use of analogy, has been omnipresent. A man desires his child to grow, therefore he chews the sprouts of the salmon berry and spits it over the child's body that it may grow as rapidly as the salmon berry. He smears the dust of mussel shells on the child's temples that it may endure as long as mussel shells. A man ties the dried navel string of

REPRINTED BY PERMISSION of the Macmillan Company from Edwin R. A. Seligman and others, editors, *Encyclopedia of the Social Sciences* 10:39–44 (New York: Macmillan, 1933). The references to this article have been omitted.

his baby boy and a woman that of her baby girl to their wrists while they are busy at highly trained occupations, so that the child will have the same proficiency in these techniques. Fish hawk eyes are rubbed over a sleeping baby's lids to give him the fish hawk's sight; and because the raven is supposed never to be sick, the raven's beak is laid by the child that it too may be free of illness. One desires the death of his enemy, therefore he stuffs a bit of the enemy's clothing down a dead snake's throat and ties it with the sinews of a corpse; he puts it in an exposed tree top and the venom of the snake and the contact with the corpse will bring about the death of the enemy.

Any analogy may be used to perform magic. Sometimes, as in Oceania, punning analogies may be employed. Often the analogies are so deeply felt and fundamental in the cultural outlook of the people that they correspond to philosophic conceptions, as in the cases where magic in agricultural practices is based on the analogy between human and plant fertility and sex is conceived to be the mystic correlate of other natural processes. The techniques may be divided into large general categories, such as Frazer's classification under the headings of sympathetic (or homeopathic, or imitative) magic and contiguous magic. They all fall into the category commonly designated as false analogies; these have been the chief reliance of all magic.

The analogies may be carried out either verbally or by imitative actions and are often carried out by both. For instance, the Chukchi of Siberia to keep a dying person alive symbolically transform a little finger into the dying man and hold it tightly in the palm. They also use traditional forms of words to express the analogies of magic; a jealous woman describes her husband as a hungry bear and her rival as the carrion he happens upon and vomits with disgust. Against evil spirits they use a simile of an impregnable ball, and they likewise exploit many other comforting figures of speech. Innumerable rites and ceremonies in all parts of the world have been built up on similar pattern setting analogies.

Magic control may also be exerted by making oneself master of some secret source of power. Egyptian name magic was of this sort; when the magician had obtained the name his control was automatic. A similar idea in primitive magic is found among the Orokaiva of New Guinea, where magic, depended upon in every situation, is strictly owned. The acts and the formulae are common knowledge, but the knowledge of the specific that gives one the power to operate magically is closely guarded. The specifics are usually leaves: a leaf that wilts immediately upon plucking to quiet the waves of a storm at sea; a leaf that grows to tremendous size to put in the water in which newborn domestic pigs are bathed; and others, with no known interpretation by analogy, which are wrapped with a bit of hair from one's enemy or buried with the yams at planting. On islands off the New Guinea mainland, as in Dobu and the Trobriands, it is the form of words constituting the spell that is the secret and guarded source of power. Amulets also usually have traditionally accepted powers, which often do not depend upon conscious analogies.

Magic procedures may be heightened in some areas by concentration, or concentration may be used alone as magic without other techniques. The person who practices the magic orders the event in his mind, with the belief that it will stage itself in reality in a like manner; the Indians of the north Pacific coast believe, for example, that by concentration they will be enabled to see quantities of dentalia and will thus come into possession of large numbers of these coveted objects.

Magic is essentially mechanistic; it is a manipulation of the external world by techniques and formulae that operate automatically. Frazer names it therefore the science of primitive man. Both magic and science are technologies, capable of being summed up in formulae and rules of procedure. Magic is believed to be, as science is, effective in its own right, in so far as its formulae are letter perfect and its routines have been complied with to the last detail; it conceives the external world to be passive and amenable to human ends as soon as the relevant techniques have been mastered. Yet not magic but the routine procedures of felling trees, knotting fish nets, tempering clay for pottery, are primitive man's literal equivalents for the knowledge classified in modern times as science. For although both magic and science are bodies of techniques, they are techniques directed to the manipulation of two incompatible worlds. Science—and in primitive life the corresponding factual knowledge and command of procedure—is directed toward the manipulation of natural phenomena operating according to cause and effect. Magic is directed toward another world operated according to another set of sequences, toward the world of the supernatural.

It is this aspect of magic which Marett has stressed. From the point of view of the forces it makes use of, the magico-religious world is a fundamental entity whose business is with power, with supercausation not with natural sequences. Marett characterizes magic as religion's disreputable sister, a value judgment that has no more validity than Frazer's opposite one of the self-respecting magician as a master of his technique and of the world, over against the cringing supplicant that religion substituted. The problem is not that of judging between the two modes of approach to the supernatural but of the recognition of the fact that magic and religion, in both Marett's and Frazer's terminology, represent two possible extremes in every type of behavior that deals with the supernatural. Magic is technological and mechanistic, a compulsion of a passive universe to one's own ends; religion is animistic behavior and employs toward a personalized universe all the kinds of behavior that hold good in human relations. In the behavior that centers around an object regarded as powerful there may be at the one extreme the magical amulet that functions automatically, that brings fortune by its mere possession and requires no honor nor humbling of one's self before it. At the opposite extreme there may be the powerful object of the type of the African fetish, which is treated essentially as if it were human; it is talked to, given presents, laid aside to recuperate when it is tired, and the crux of its use is the rapport between the operator and the sacred bundle. In techniques of inducing power by the spoken word there are likewise, on the one hand, the formulae and abracadabra that achieve their end automatically and, on the other, the prayers of the saint who puts himself into intimate relationship with his god. In witchcraft the jinn controlled may come automatically at the rubbing of Aladdin's lamp, or a sorcerer may maintain relationship with the devil that serves because of offerings, intercourse and prostration. Functionally therefore magic cannot be discussed without its complement, religion; they are always alternative techniques for inducing power and for achieving luck by means other than those of the natural cause and effect sequences. A people may have little magic and yet its conduct may be saturated with animistic techniques by which the same sort of supernatural sanction is achieved that in another region is achieved by magical practices. Both the animistic and magical techniques, however, have in common the fact that they rely upon wish fulfilments rather than upon mundane labor in order to attain their ends.

The mental confusion which gives rise to magic is different from that in which animistic beliefs have flourished. The latter result from a lack of distinction between the animate and the inanimate world and a consequent carrying over of human relations into man's dealings with the non-human. Magic, on the other hand, in all its branches is the consequence of a blindness to the essential disparateness of techniques that can be used in dealing with the various aspects of the natural world. It teaches, for example, that a treatment of the sword which has caused the wound will cure the wound, or that milk can be made to sour properly by treating the sacred cowbell. The fallacy involved is the ignoring of the fact that every end in nature has its own techniques by which it can be achieved and the assumption of a mystic sympathy in the external universe by which techniques applied at one point are efficacious at another point. Progress in control of the universe has always been furthered by giving up pantheistic procedures and limiting techniques strictly to specific ends.

The confusion of thought involved in magic has been emphasized by Lévy-Bruhl as the essential fact in the working of the primitive mind, which he has designated as prelogical in contrast with the reasoning processes of modern man. He concludes from primitive practices in regard to birth and death, omens, dreams, divination, tabu, warfare and curing that primitives do not make logical distinctions. More categorically he contends that in totemism the primitive man does not know himself from the eponymous animal and in relation to the dead he does not know the ghost from the living. It can, however, be shown from the testimony of the most primitive magicians that they are quite able to make these distinctions. They are merely acting upon a basic philosophical creed which, if it were explicitly phrased, would be similar to that of the mediaeval doctrine of the macrocosm and the microcosm which assumes that existence of a mystic sympathy pervading the universe, thus making facts observable or brought to pass in one field significant and operative also in another.

Magical ideas and procedures are plentiful in contemporary civilization. The secularization of modern life has proceeded at the expense of religion and its gods rather than at the expense of magic. Animism and the personalization of the external universe have been banned from sophisticated thinking and children are now induced to outgrow their tendencies in this direction as soon as possible. Comparable advance toward non-supernatural behavior has not been made, however, in the realm of magical procedures. Those who have shaken themselves loose from the trammels of religious tradition often swell the ranks of the various divinatory cults based on the fundamental assumptions of magic—a clientele of Wall Street investors depends upon the verdict of astrologers, and air pilots skilled in the latest triumphs of mechanical science guide their acts by signs. There are innumerable more subtle beliefs in modern civilization that are essentially magical; those that are partially discarded are easier to isolate than those that are still accepted. The traditional American scheme of education is distinctly magical; it does not attempt to draw up a program of what the child will need as an adult and direct its attention to the specific necessary techniques. Its method can be justified only by faith in a magical oneness in the intellectual world; education is regarded as power in the non-naturalistic sense. Modern society is still operating magically with most of the difficult problems that have to do with sex; that is, it does not recognize that there are adjustments and desirable ends in the field of sex which should be achieved apart from all dogmas of revealed religion or traditional morality. Few countries have as yet effectively acted upon the belief that good results in the control of industrial problems or international trade follow only from intelligent and specific procedures accurately adjusted to specific problems. The most characteristic magic of present western civilization is that which centers around property; the violent sense of loss that is experienced by the typical modern in the loss of a sum of money, quite irrespective of whether he and his family will be housed and clothed and fed, is as much a case of magical identification of the ego with externals as any of Lévy-Bruhl's examples of prelogical mentality.

Magic, being essentially only a supernaturalistic rule of thumb procedure, may be either traditionally developed or almost neglected in any field of culture. The contrast between American Indian cultures and those of western Melanesia in this respect is very great. The magic practices of the Kwakiutl are on a level with modern superstitions; they give good luck and are not neglected, but they exist quite apart from the main concerns of the culture. A chief seeking to consolidate his prestige engages in many pertinent activities; he may incidentally employ the services of a proprietor of magic techniques, but his activities are not directed to any great extent by the magic that may be used, nor is it essential that he employ magic at all. The religious practitioner, the shaman, operates not by virtue of magic techniques but because of his rapport with a guardian spirit to which he has not only a personal right through a validating experience but also an inherited right as a member of his family group.

On the other hand, on the island of Dobu, as Fortune has shown, magic practices cover every phase of life and are considered indispensable. There routine procedures are believed to be inadequate in all human activities, and the acquisition of magic is therefore the foremost concern of every ambitious man. It is categorically denied that gardens, the source of the food supply, can grow without magic, despite the fact that the gardens of white settlers have grown for two generations. The great care given to the gardens is a magical routine to keep a man's yams in his own garden and to lure away as many of his neighbor's yams as his magic can accomplish. Every man's gains are regarded as another man's losses, and magic is the chief reliance in every individual's endeavor to succeed at the cost of his neighbor. A man's harvest from his garden is therefore evidence of his magical prowess and as such is suspect. Harvest is the occasion of most carefully preserved privacy; no one outside the immediate family is allowed to see a family's magically acquired gains. Sex intercourse is likewise regarded as the result of successful magic that gives one power over another man's woman, a conception which is widespread. The asocial nature of Dobuan magic is strikingly illustrated in the use of disease bearing spells in the validation of the ownership of betel nut, coconut palm and other trees. Magic is used also for rain making, for success in economic exchange on the *kula* and in legal actions of all kinds and for causing illness and death to one's opponents. Only in reference to pregnancy do the Dobuans recognize naturalistic causation; they understand it to come about naturally as a result of impregnation. The neighboring Trobrianders have prevented such an anomaly in the general theory of magic; they deny biological paternity and foster a belief which would have brought about a complete consistency in magical world outlook were it found in Dobu. Magic therefore according to the constellation of beliefs into which it enters may be, as in Dobu, a primary concern in social situations and the indispensable guaranty of success or it may be an unimportant adjunct to achievement.

It is not helpful to make clean cut classifications of black and white magic except in cases where the local culture has elaborated a dualism on this basis. The dualism is always possible and has sometimes been made among primitive peoples, but usually magic is not definitely committed either to good or to bad but is used for either as occasion arises. There is no way, for example, to distinguish good magic from the black art in Dobu, where the use of magic for gardens is regarded as achieving yams as spoils and the cures for disease carry with them inalienably the spells that cause it.

The province of magic cannot be regarded as limited to any one field of human behavior. In support of the hypothesis that magic practice is confined to dangerous activities not amenable to matter of fact control Malinowski instances the Melanesians' application of magic to seafaring in canoes, to weather techniques and to pregnancy control. Many other examples could be given of the use of magic in times of peril. On the other hand, a list of occasions in which magic is used without danger being present could also be compiled. One of the characteristic magic practices of Hawaii, for example, was the supernatural consecration of the home, a rite in which the birth of a child was taken as an analogy, a bit of thatch being left free to be cut as the navel cord at the ritual housewarming. The magical procedure in the Toda dairy does not mean that the preparation of sour milk products is more precarious there than it is in other cattle regions where dairying is quite matter of fact, as among the Yakut. Similarly, if danger were the soil of magic one would expect a correlation of magical agricultural procedures with environments difficult for or unsuited to the growing of plants; on the contrary, however, such magic is most luxuriantly developed in the tropical island region of the Papuans, and agriculture was probably never carried on under less hazardous conditions. The contention of Hubert and Mauss that magic is the proscribed use of supernatural power, the illicit over against the accepted, is also an interpretation based on very local conditions and is inadequate in the light of what is at present known of the nature of magic in many primitive regions. On the contrary, it has become evident that the province of magic in human societies is as wide as human desires.

Magic has often been interpreted as a salutary influence in human development. Malinowski has held that magic serves as a remedy for specific maladjustments and mental conflicts in that it "prescribes the adequate idea, standardizes the valuable emotional tone and establishes a line of conduct which carries man over the dangerous moment . . . it supplies most of the co-ordinating and driving forces of labour, it develops the qualities of forethought, of order, of steadiness and punctuality, which are essential to all successful enterprise." Recently Kempf has still further elaborated the argument by holding that magic beliefs "are psycho-therapeutic efforts to make easier the stresses of physiological functioning in a social environment" and that "man grew his cultural ways and beliefs [in magic] in order to control these [physiological] functions, just as the pains of hunger pressed him to hoard food." Any group may use magic, as it may use any sanction, to build up socially desirable activities; and the people Malinowski is describing, the Trobriands, with their pregnancy magic and their magical treatment of economic exchange in courtship terms, have done so in a decided manner. But a wider survey of the subject merely emphasizes the fact that in such a culture as that of the Trobriands social drives in the use of magic have become stronger than asocial ones. The fact that some societies have used magic for beneficent social purposes must be regarded not as revealing the primary role of magic but as an example of the way in which these societies have been able to direct cultural traits to their special purposes.

Magic has also been held to be a valuable human support as an effective emotional release; it is argued that it has prevented dangerous repressions and made for the health of the social body. This emotional release is evident, for example, in the Chukchi formulae and in the Dobuan realistic imitations of death which accompany the use of a disease charm. No actual killing of the enemy could be so satisfactory in details of vindictiveness as the pre-enactment that is staged in the interests of magic by the Algonquian medicine man. These emotionally satisfying compensations are, however, less common over the world than one would suppose a priori. The techniques of magic are more devious. The emotional satisfaction is by no means direct and vehement; it seems most often swamped in a meticulous observance of petty rules. For the most part, directly because of its character as a mechanical control, magic is cold, technical and non-emotional, a rule of thumb procedure, and it is difficult to regard it as a satisfactory compensatory emotional release.

Freud has emphasized the parallel between the mechanisms of magic and those of obsessional neuroses; both are explained in terms of system formations by which fundamental displacements are achieved that supersede reality for the persons concerned and involve "motor hallucinations" and even "a fundamental renunciation of the satisfaction of inherent instincts." The role of wish fulfilment must be freely admitted; it is a factor not only in the development of magic but in all cultural traits. The world man actually lives in—in the sense of his inescapable necessities and the inevitable conditions of life—always bulks very small in relation to the world he makes for himself. Magic is used to build up these worlds and to give security within them. Nevertheless, magic is only, in Tylor's terms, an occult science and a strong development of occultism may indicate extreme insecurity as often as it indicates security. The yam magic does not give agricultural security in Dobu; on the contrary, it emphasizes a danger spot in the culture and far from minimizing this stress in a community in which food is scarce it institutionalizes it. Security in agriculture seems to prevail under such conditions as exist in the Trobriands, where magic has fastened itself upon other objectives of life and where agriculture is a naturalistic occupation in comparison with its practice in Dobu. Magic potency ascribed to menstruating women or to the dead has not generally inculcated social security in relation to these portents; it has rather indicated the situations which a culture regards as social hazards. The analogy with neurotic behavior is striking; whether or not a culture has chosen to regard women or persons recently dead as supernaturally dangerous, the usual course has been to erect in a neurotic manner an associated edifice of ceremonial by means of which displacement is achieved and the object of dread pushed off the scene or brought back in some more acceptable guise.

The role of magic in institutionalizing fear reactions is especially marked in witchcraft. This is clearest in situations where sorcery as a body of known and recognized magical procedures does not exist but is nevertheless an inescapable fear and a common accusation. The Salem witch trials were evidently of this type, as were the contemporary English anti-witch demonstrations. Primitive cultures, such as that of the Pueblo Indians of the southwestern United States, use witchcraft in analogous ways; the fear of sorcery is a motivation in every situation in life, but no spells or rites actually practiced by intending sorcerers have been uncovered, and it seems probable that they do not exist. Even in regions where magic as an objectification of panic is balanced by its use as a control over the external world, the social control it exercises is characteristically through the institutionalizing of a fear neurosis. In Australia, for example, there are traditional techniques associated with the art of "pointing the bone," but its social significance is not so much in the fact that a few old men make use of the practice to inflict punishment as in the fact that it is the social setting for the neurosis of a conviction of death that can rarely be dislodged; entire villages have died in the strength of this conviction.

Thus the contention that magic has had a salutary role in human history must be balanced by facts which present it in a different light. Far from being an asset it has often been a heavy liability, and its phenomena are analogous to the delusions of grandeur and fear constructs of the neurotic. Its procedures are in psychiatric terminology mechanisms of displacement, and they tend in both primitive and modern societies to substitute unreal achievement for real.

An Introduction to Zuni Mythology [1]

✤ Folkloristic studies, since the days of Cosquin and the students stimulated by the collections of the Grimm brothers, have been extensive

REPRINTED BY PERMISSION of the Columbia University Press from *Zuni Mythology*, 2 vols., Columbia University Contributions to Anthropology, No. 21 (New York: Columbia University Press, 1935) 1:xi–xliii. In its present form, previously published in *An Anthropologist at Work*, pp. 226–45, the Introduction has been condensed by approximately one-third.
[1] The principal references for this study are: F. H. Cushing, *Zuni Folk Tales* (New York: Putnam's, 1901); M. C. Stevenson, The Zuni Indians, *Twenty-third Annual Report of the Bureau of American Ethnology* (Washington, 1904), pp. 1–634; Ruth Bunzel, Introduction to Zuni Ceremonialism, *Forty-seventh Annual Report of the Bureau of American Ethnology* (Washington, 1932), pp. 467–544.

rather than intensive. Whether the proposed problem was historical reconstruction or a study of creative processes in mythology, the method that has been followed is that of far-flung comparative studies. This method has been used by Ehrenreich and the psycho-analytic students of myth, both of whom are interested in the role of symbolism in folklore, as well as by the modern school of Aarne, which is interested in reconstructing archetypal forms of folktales, and by students like Bolte and Polívka who are committed simply to documenting distribution.

The intensive study of one body of folklore has been scanted throughout the history of folkloristic studies, and little stress has been laid upon its possible rewards. The most valuable studies of this kind have tabled and analyzed the cultural behavior embodied in the tales, and these have been made only in American Indian material, i.e. Franz Boas' "Description of the Tsimshian Based on Their Mythology" [2]; Franz Boas' *Kwakiutl Culture as Reflected in Their Mythology* [3]; and Clara Ehrlich's "Tribal Culture in Crow Mythology." [4] Such studies show the great amount of cultural material in myth, and stress the value of folklore for an understanding of the culture. This is not the only kind of intensive study of folklore. Boas has defined, and contrasted with other regions, the themes of Eskimo folklore in "The Folklore of the Eskimo." [5] He has indicated the relation of these themes to the cultural behavior and ideals among that people. In addition, there is also the possibility of the study of the native narrator, that is, the literary materials which he has at his disposal and his handling of them. [6]

These problems have seldom been attacked, and several circumstances have contributed to this neglect on the part of folklore students. In the first place, the most striking and obvious result of research in the early days of folkloristic study was always the fantastically wide distribution of episodes and plots, and everyone therefore joined in diffusion studies.

[2] *Thirty-first Annual Report of the Bureau of American Ethnology* (Washington, 1916), pp. 29–1037.
[3] Memoirs of the American Folk-Lore Society, No. 28 (New York, 1935).
[4] *Journal of American Folk-Lore* 46:128 (1933).
[5] *Journal of American Folk-Lore* 17:1–13 (1904); see also Ralph L. Briggs, The Hero in the Folk Tales of Spain, Germany and Russia, *Journal of American Folk-Lore* 44:27–42 (1931).
[6] See, for a comparative study, Dorothy Demetracopoulou, The Loon Woman: A Study in Synthesis, *Journal of American Folk-Lore* 46:1–128 (1933).

In the second place, there are certain conditions which must be fulfilled before intensive study of one body of folklore can yield any considerable fruits, and these conditions have not often been met in the available collections. For the most profitable study of single bodies of mythology, folktales should hold an important place in the tribal life, not being relegated, for example, to children's amusement or used solely as word-perfect recitations of magical formulae; a large body of tales should have been recorded, and over as long a period as possible; the culture of the people who tell the tales should be well known; and folklore among that people should be a living and functioning culture trait.

These optimum conditions are fulfilled in the folklore of Zuñi, the largest pueblo of the Southwest of the United States. Even compared with other North American tribes, mythology is a highly developed and serious art in Zuñi, and the great number of tales that have been collected by many different persons extend over a period of fifty years. The culture of Zuñi is well known, and in discussing the tales I have been able to use my own first-hand acquaintance with Zuñi beliefs and behavior, as well as detailed accounts by other students. Finally, in contrast to that of almost all other tribes of the North American continent, folklore in Zuñi is not moribund. The processes that can be studied in it are not reconstructed in a kind of folkloristic archaeology but are open to observation and experiment.

When these conditions can be fulfilled, intensive study of a single body of folklore is of first-rate theoretical importance, whether the problem at issue is historical reconstruction, the study of culture, or literary problems in the development of oral traditions. It seems obvious enough that studies in the two latter problems can be carried out best by careful intensive study, and that the students of symbolism, for example, have overlooked in favor of misleading comparative studies a method of work which can yield definite results. Even in the matter of historical reconstruction, which is the chief end of comparative studies of folklore, intensive study has much to contribute. The usual library-trained comparative student works with standard versions from each locality; in primitive cultures, usually one from a tribe. This version arbitrarily becomes "the" tribal tale, and is minutely compared with equally arbitrary standard tales from other tribes. But in such a body of mythology as that of Zuñi, many different variants coexist, and the different forms these variants take cannot be ascribed to different historical levels, or even in large measure to particular tribal contacts, but are different literary combinations of incidents in different plot sequences. The comparative student may well learn from intensive studies not to point an argument that would be invalidated if half a dozen quite different versions from the same tribe were placed on record.

The two problems which I shall consider at the present time from the analysis of Zuñi mythology are: I, the themes which their folklore elaborates and the relation of these to their culture; II, the literary problems of the Zuñi narrator.

I

No folktale is generic. It is always the tale of one particular people with one particular livelihood and social organization and religion. The final form that a tale takes in that culture is influenced, often fundamentally, by attitudes and customs that cannot be discovered except with full knowledge of life and behavior among that people. It has always been obvious to students of every theoretical persuasion that folklore tallied with culture and yet did not tally with it, and the majority of students have agreed upon one convenient explanation of those instances where the two are at odds. Folklore, it is said, reflects not the customs and beliefs of the narrators of the tales, but those of many generations past; cultural survivals of earlier ages are perpetuated in folklore, and these, it is often felt, are the chief reason for the study of oral traditions. Even conditions of barbarism in which fathers are supposed to have eaten their children, and conditions of primal life when man first gained ascendancy over animals, have been said to be embalmed in folklore.

A conservatism that perpetuates long-discarded customs, however, is characteristic of a dead lore rather than a living one, and the great emphasis on the importance of survivals in the interpretation of folklore is evidently due to certain characteristics of oral tradition in Western civilization. European folklore was rescued from the memories of old men and women much of that as the Plains Indians is rescued today. It was recorded by collectors long after its heyday. Grimm's tales are found to reflect the manners and customs of the feudal age, not contemporary contacts with industrialism or with urban civilization, and the belief has become current that survivals of old customs are perpetuated in folklore through great lapses of time. This, however, is to generalize the senescence of folklore into a law by means of which mythology is elaborately interpreted. Folklore often remains current and can be adequately collected when it is no longer a living trait. North American Indians can almost always relate their folktales long after their aboriginal cultural life is in abeyance, and many valuable bodies of mythology have been collected in dead cultures from old men who learned the stories in their youth. The functioning of myth in culture and the processes of cultural adaptation, however, cannot be adequately studied in these cases. Comparison of variants under such conditions indicates mainly how much or how little different informants have forgotten of a dead culture trait, and such comparison is comparative unrewarding. In Zuñi tales are constantly told, and recounting folktales is an habitual occupation of a great number of the most important members of the community.

A living folklore, such as that of Zuñi, reflects the contemporary interests and judgments of its tellers, and adapts incidents to its own cultural usages. Like any cultural trait, folklore tends, of course, to perpetuate traditional forms, and there is a certain lag in folklore as there is in contemporary statecraft or in morals. But the scope of this conservatism is limited in folklore as in other traits. It is never sufficient to give us license to reconstruct the items of a racial memory; and contemporary attitudes are always to be reckoned with, rather than those that have been superseded in that culture. In the present collection the cultural lag is apparent in many details of overt behavior. In the folktales, for example, except in those recognized by the tellers as Mexican, entrance to the house is by means of a ladder to the roof and down another ladder from the hatchway, yet doors have been common in Zuñi since 1888 and are today universal except in the kivas. Old conditions, therefore, have been equally retained in the ceremonial house and in the folktale. The same may be said of the use of stone knives. Stone knives are still laid upon altars and used in ceremonies; and in folktales also heroes use stone knives instead of the omnipresent contemporary store knife. More elaborate modern innovations are also unrecognized in folklore. At present sheep herding occupies much of the life of Zuñi men, and hunting is in abeyance. In the tales, however, all heroes are hunters, and there is no mention of sheep herding except in tales recognized as Mexican. In like manner men do not now come courting with a bundle of gifts for the girl, but in folklore this is a convention usually observed. Similarly, at the present time the activity of the medicine societies is centered in their great all-night ceremony at the winter solstice, the individual planting of prayer-sticks at full moon, and in not very exacting incidental activities. In the myths, on the other hand, every member goes every night to his medicine society and returns home when others are in bed.

The cultural lag that is represented by these differences between custom in contemporary life and in folktales covers, however, a short period, and by no means gives indication of an early cultural horizon such as can be reconstructed, for instance, from comparative studies of culture, still less from studies of comparative linguistics. The agreement between the conduct of contemporary life and the picture of life in the folktales is very close. The roles of men and women in Zuñi life, the role of the priest-hoods, the conduct of sex life, the concern with witchcraft are all faithfully indicated.

Where there is a contrast between Zuñi custom and literary convention, the divergence commonly rests upon other considerations than survival of older customs. Even in the divergences just mentioned, cultural lag is not a sufficient explanation. It may well be, as any native will assure you, that, in times not long past, men spent every night in their medicine society meetings. On the other hand, it is possible that in those times as in these, this was a conventional description of a golden age, and golden ages have often existed only in the imagination. The impulse to idealize must be reckoned with in folkloristic contrasts with contemporary life when it is also possible to set the difference down to cultural lag. Similarly, courting with bundles may not be a survival of an older custom but a borrowed incident which is a folkloristic convention. Stone knives and entrance through the hatchway also have become conventional attributes of a less troubled and ideal age, and from this point of view should be considered along with the fabulous prowess of heroes as runners in the stick race.

This tendency to idealize in folklore has often been pointed out. There is another set of discrepancies in Zuñi folklore that cannot so easily be disposed of. The most striking instance is that of the constant recurrence of polygamy in the tales. Zuñi institutions are thoroughly monogamous. It is of course conceivable that the folkloristic pattern reproduces earlier conditions. Polygamy is allowed almost everywhere in North America outside the Southwest and even polyandry is accepted in certain nearby tribes. The absence of any taboo against multiple spouses is an old and general North American Indian trait. To assign the Zuñi folkloristic pattern, however, to such a reflection of an earlier background is difficult for two reasons. In the first place, all pueblo cultures have the Zuñi taboo on polygamy and pueblo culture is exceedingly old and stable, as one may judge from archaeological evidence in material culture. It is doubtful whether any folklore can be cited from any part of the world that reflects cultural conditions as remote as those before pueblo culture took form, and there is, therefore, good reason for dissatisfaction with this explanation. In the second place, even if it were possible to interpret the Zuñi folkloristic pattern of polygamy as a survival, we should still have to explain why the marriage with eight wives or with two husbands is prominent in Zuñi mythology and not generally over North America. The simultaneous marriage with many wives was culturally allowed over most of the continent, but it does not figure in their tales as it does in pueblo folklore. The presumption that is indicated by a study of the distribution of this folkloristic pattern in North America is that in the pueblos polygamy is a grandiose folkloristic convention partaking on the one hand of usual mythological exaggeration and on the other of a compensatory daydream. Just as the hero of folktales kills a buck every day, or four in a single day, so he also is courted by eight maidens and marries them. When a hero is given supernatural power by his supernatural father, he signalizes it by accepting all eight of the priests' daughters who had flouted him, killing them, and resuscitating them to serve his triumph. It is a grandiose demonstration of power, and of the same nature as the rain-blessing the eight wives bring back to the pueblo after their resuscitation, a blessing so great that the consequent flood fills the whole valley and the people have to escape to the top of the mesa. In the same way the hunter whose sister uses her supernatural power in his behalf marries wives from all the seven towns, and in his witch wife's reprisal she has him abducted by eight Crane girls who keep him as their husband for four years. Marriage with many wives is a Zuñi fantasy of the same order as raising the dead or traveling with seven-league boots in other bodies of folklore. It plays a fairytale role in Zuñi mythology which is automatically rendered impossible in those areas of North America where tales of polygamy and polyandry have bases in fact. What compensatory elements the tale embodies it is hard to prove, but it seems likely that these are present.

Other contrasts between custom and folkloristic conventions must be explained as fundamentally compensatory. The abandonment of children at birth is a constantly recurring theme and is alien to Zuñi custom. In real life it does not come up for consideration at all. Illegitimate children are cared for in their mothers' homes, and present-day gossips, though they specialize in outrageous libels, do not tell of any instance in which an infant has been done away with. All men and women, not only the parents, give children the fondest care. There is no cultural background for the abandonment of illegitimate children. It is harder to judge about the abandonment of young children in famine. The tales of migrations to pueblos where crops have not failed are based on fact and such incidents may possibly have occurred, where children too large to carry and too young to make the journey were left behind, though actual reminiscences are always of tender protection of the child. The incidents, however, of the girl in childbed who overtakes her party, leaving the baby in the grinding stone, are regarded as fabulous by contemporary Zuñis, like all tales of women who are able to get up immediately after childbirth as if nothing had happened. The abandonment of the child and the impossible physical recovery are grouped in one category. When the story of babies abandoned at birth is used in explanation of Zuñi custom, the narrator concludes from the incident: "That's why girls who become pregnant before marriage conceal their condition"—which is true—not "That's why they expose their babies."

The fact remains that abandonment of children is an extraordinarily popular theme in Zuñi folklore. The clue lies in the fact that the hearers' identification is with the child, not with the mother. Even women, who would be expected to identify with the mother in telling these tales, comment on the reunion of the abandoned child with his mother from the point of view of the child. "He made her cry all right," a woman said

122

with heat, and, "Oh, she (the mother) was *ashamed*." The plots are all concerned with the supernatural assistance and human success of the poor child, and often the whole plot is directed toward the triumph of the abandoned child over the mother or the parents. In the popular tale of the *Deserted children protected by dragonfly* the parents return in poverty and miserably sue their children for favors. The daydream, from the point of view of the child, is completed by the final largess of the children and their appointment to priestly rank. In two versions of the *Twin Children of the Sun*, the twins return, make a laughingstock of their mother, and force her to confess. These two versions, which tell of the children's abandonment at birth, contrast strongly with two other versions, in which the girl does not expose her children but is killed by a witch or by the priests as a punishment for her unconfessed pregnancy. Her sons therefore do not humiliate her, but vindicate their mother's memory. The point of the story is entirely different.

The popularity of the theme of abandoned children in Zuñi has a psychological significance that parallels the familiar daydreams of children in our civilization which detail their parents' suffering at their imminent death. That is, it is the expression of a resentment directed by children against their parents and worked out into a daydream of the children's imagined vantage.

Another theme, which also reflects Zuñi culture but with a difference is that of violent action based upon secret enmity. Grudges are cherished in Zuñi. They are usually the rather generalized expression of slights and resentments in a small community. In actual life they give rise to malicious aspersions, but in folklore they are usually satisfied by nothing less than the death of the offender. People grudge others their prosperity and set about to destroy them; they grudge a man his success in hunting and attempt to do away with him; they are jealous of a supernatural who has brought a new dance to Zuñi and try to bewitch him; a priest who has not been paid for instruction kills the delinquent; the child who is scolded for shirking satisfies her grudge by leaving so that her family fears she is dead and recover her only after search by the supernaturals; people are angry because a girl will not lend a dipper and they have to drink from their hands, therefore a feud starts and two girls are killed. Men and women both resent any slight in courtship; the woman tries to kill the man who has refused her a piece of his game (a usual courtship gesture in the tales), and men kill or bewitch girls who have laughed at them, or refused them a drink (a courtship preliminary today as well). The deserted husband ritualistically causes a drought, an earthquake, or an epidemic, which threatens to wipe out the whole pueblo. The deserted wife similarly summons Navahoes or Apaches to demolish the village, or attempts to kill her husband. Unlike those of the Plains, Zuñi folkways have no place for an ideal of character which overlooks slights, however small, and their folktales provide exaggerated fantasies of reprisal. In a culture in which homicide occurs with such extraordinary rarity that instances are not even remembered, the compensatory violence of these reprisals is the more striking.

True to the peculiar ideology of Zuñi these reprisals are easily phrased as "teaching people to love you," i.e. to act decently toward you. The despised children, whom the people spit at, throwing refuse and urine into their grandmother's house, get the help of Salt Mother who takes away all the clothing in the pueblo. They tell her: "The people at Itiwana hate us. We want them to learn to love us." The people have to stay in bed all the time and in their shame are brought to the point of begging work from the poor children. The latter remove the curse when the people promise to "love them." The whole story is an excellent illustration of the strange way in which, according to Zuñi notions, you teach people to love you.

Zuñi folklore, therefore, in those cases where it does not mirror contemporary custom, owes its distortions to various fanciful exaggerations and compensatory mechanisms. The role of daydreams, of wish fulfillment, is not limited to these cases of distortion. It is equally clear in the tales that most minutely reflect the contemporary scene. Zuñi folklore differs from most North American Indian mythology in that the usual daydream is little concerned with prowess in warfare. Nor are there in Zuñi accounts of supernatural encounters and the acquisition of power, such as fill the folktales of the Plains Indians. Zuñi folktales are as faithful to Zuñi fantasies in what they exclude as in what they include. Their most popular theme is the triumph of the despised and weak and previously worsted. The poor orphan boy is victorious in hunting, in stick races, in gambling, and in courtship; those who do not have witch power are triumphant over those who have; the stunted ragamuffin Ahaiyute win first place in everything.

There is singular mildness in Zuñi tales, and this mildness is strangely at variance with the compensatory violence we have already discussed in the reprisal stories which have cherished grudges as their theme. In these latter the violence of the daydream is fabulous, and the very fact that it is not a reflection of Zuñi behavior allows the vengeance to take the most extreme forms. In other tales the mildness of actual Zuñi life and institutions are accurately reflected. The idea of trapping all the witches into an ambush from which they could kill Apaches and must therefore have to become bow priests is a curious one. "So A·lucpa caught all the witches in the bow priesthood. They were forced to go into retreat and be purified. They were bow priests. Only one witch had not been able to go out. So one witch was left. That is why there is no witch society any more, because A·lucpa made them all bow priests." This tale in no way calls in question the great prestige of the bow priesthood in Zuñi, nor the fear and hatred of witches. Nevertheless the conclusion is felt as adequate. In a case of personal vengeance, the priest's son who has been distressed at his wife's demonstrativeness calls the Apache to kill him in order to test his wife's faithfulness to his memory. She is merely left to enjoy herself at the favorite yaya dance, by which he proves her affection was too shallow to allow for proper respect for her husband. "He turned into an eagle, and that is why we value eagle feathers."

II

The literary problems which confront a primitive narrator are easily misunderstood. The gap between the traditionalism of primitive mythology and the emphasis upon originality in our own literature is so great that the reader from our civilization confronted by a collection of folktales is often led to false conclusions. Many students have assumed that the fixity of the tales is absolute or almost so, that the individual narrator has no literary problems, and that the tales originated in a mystical source called communal authorship. On the other hand, it would be as easy to interpret the tales as far more fortuitous than they really are, for from the point of view of the outsider the incidents out of which the tale is built might just as well be other incidents, the stylistic elements might as well be omitted or amplified in any imaginable direction. In fact, because of the diffuseness and ease of prose, it is far easier to mistake the problems of the artist in this field than, for instance, in the plastic arts.

There is no more communal authorship in folklore than there is a communal designer in ironwork or a communal priest in religious rites. The whole problem is unreal. There is no conceivable source of any cultural trait other than the behavior of some man, woman or child. What is communal about the process is the social acceptance by which the trait becomes a part of the teaching handed down to the next generation. The role of the narrator in such a body of folklore as that of Zuñi remains as real as that of any storyteller in any civilization though its scope is somewhat changed by the role of the audience.

On the other hand, even more serious misunderstanding of folklore is introduced by the outsider's inability to appreciate the fixed limits within which the narrator works. The artist works within definite traditional limits as truly in folklore as in music. The first requisite in understanding any folk literature is to recognize the boundaries within which he operates.

In Zuñi, tales fall into no clearly distinguishable categories. Even the Emergence story, which is the Zuñi scripture, is not reserved for the priests nor owned by them. It is freely repeated by any fireside by any layman, and all versions differ markedly, not so much in order of incidents as in the details introduced. Incidents of it, moreover, can be lifted and used as the basis of entertaining stories.

Tales of kachinas, also, form no special group. Kachinas are freely introduced even into European tales, and are heroes of romances who marry several wives, contest with witches, and win in stick races. Much of the stock saga of the Ahaiyute has evidently been ascribed to them since Cushing's day, and these little supernatural twins figure as supernatural helpers in tales of every kind. They make themselves a "kapitan" and buy a dog from a Mexican in a patently Mexican tale. In other cases the Ahaiyute tales are direct transcriptions of Zuñi daydreams and represent the wish fulfillments most desired by the people. A variety of stories are attributed to the Ahaiyute in one of several versions, and it seems probable that this tendency is still operative in Zuñi. If that is true, still other stories that were not yet told of the twins ten years ago when these stories were collected may become Ahaiyute stories in the future.

It is in keeping with the fact that folklore is such a living and popular trait in Zuñi at the present time that tales of European derivation are so little differentiated from others. The ones that are popular or have been told for some time or are retold by a good narrator often mirror the details of Zuñi life to the last degree. Cushing fifty years ago published an excellent example of this in his day in the tale of *The Cock and the Mouse*, which adapted an Italian accumulative tale he had himself repeated in Zuñi.[7]

Animal trickster tales, which form so large a bulk of many North American mythologies, are little told.

In all tales, therefore, since the short animal incident occurs so rarely, roughly the same objectives are present to the narrator. Of these stylistic aims, probably the one most relied upon is the endless incorporation of cultural details. In most mythologies the picture of cultural life that can be abstracted from the tales, as in the studies of the Tsimshian, Kwakiutl, and Crow, is a comparatively adequate description of most phases of social life, but in Zuñi there is in addition a loving reiteration of detail that is over and above this faithful rendition. The most extreme examples are the long descriptions of ceremonies. These have practically no plot but are strung together on some thread such as that of the Pekwin who grieved for his dead wife and was comforted by each of the three religious organizations of Zuñi, which each brought out a dance in turn, and finally by the great ceremony of the Corn Dance. In one of these ceremonies more than forty participants in the dance are severally invited by the bow priests to take part. In each of the forty retellings the priests go to the individual's house, greet those who live there with the conventional greeting, "How have you lived these days, my fathers, my mothers, my children?" are answered, fed, thank them for the food, explain the part in the dance they wish them to assume and conduct them back to the priests' chamber or leave them to prepare for the occasion. In each case, also, the moment's occupations of the principal occupants of the room

[7] Cushing, *Zuni Folk Tales*, p. 411.

127

are described as the priests enter. Practice for the dancing and the great occasion itself are meticulously described in the same fashion.

The Zuñi narrator, besides this general preoccupation, has a special obligation to relate certain details. The greeting formulas, with the offer of food to the visitor and his thanks, recur constantly. Localization is imperative, and certain places are the scenes of certain kinds of incidents, as Cunte'kaia is the scene of witch tales and Hecokta of ogre tales.

Indication of points of the compass is marked, but is much less of a stylistic necessity than in the pueblo tales from Laguna, for instance. The introduction of helpful animals is marked in all tales where such incidents are relevant. Such animals, according to their abilities, fly, gnaw, or kill, for the hero. Stylistic obliviousness to incisiveness or condensation is obvious in all the tales and if anything is only the more marked in the text translations.

The Zuñi narrator is almost always free to incorporate his special knowledge in a tale. If he has taken part in a Corn Dance, his incidents of the Corn Dance reproduce his own experience, which is then retold by others. Men, as well as women, incorporate accounts of woman's childbirth ritual, or of cooking techniques. The Emergence tale is used as a basis for the incorporation of a variety of ritual with which a narrator is familiar.

Cushing's tale of *The Cock and the Mouse* has already been mentioned. It is a striking example of the extent to which Zuñi stylistic requirements operate to remodel a borrowed tale. He himself told a group of native friends a European accumulative tale and a year later recorded the same tale as he heard it told by one of his listeners. The European tale tells simply of the joint nut-gathering adventure of the cock and the mouse. When the cock had tried in vain to reach the nuts he asked the mouse to throw some down to him, and the nut cut the cock's head. He ran to an old woman to get it bandaged, and she asked two hairs for payment. He ran to the dog for these, who asked bread. He went to the baker, who asked wood, to the forest, which asked water. He went to the fountain, which gave him water, and so he retraced his steps and got his head bound up. The story is bare of all further details. In keeping with Zuñi narrative standards, the adapted version begins with a description of the old woman and her turkey yard, "like an eagle cage against a wall."

The cock of the original story has appropriately enough become a Zuñi pet turkey, and the fact that the turkey has a beard while the cock has not is capitalized in the resulting story. The old woman had only the one turkey and she was too poor to give it meat, so that the turkey was always meat-hungry. One day he caught sight of Mouse's tail disappearing in his hole and snapped it up for a worm. Now the mouse's tail was his "sign of manhood" and he vowed vengeance. So far the additions are by way of supplying the traditional literary motivation of the despised and put-upon who set out to overcome their enemies. The mouse, therefore, made friends with the cock, who allowed him to eat crumbs thrown him by the old woman, and finally brought the turkey a nut out of his own hoard. The turkey lamented that he was not free like the mouse to gather such nuts and the mouse offered to gnaw the fastening of his corral. This incident is the familiar *Helpful Animals*: rodent (mouse, gopher, etc.) gnaws (ropes, wall, tree roots, etc.). When the nut hit the turkey he was stunned, fell "dead" as the Zuñis say, and the mouse avenged himself by gnawing off his neck bristles, his "signs of manhood," in exact compensation for what he had himself suffered. When the turkey could get up he went to the woman to have his head bound and she asked him for four neck bristles, i.e. his signs of manhood. But they had been gnawed off. He therefore went to the dog, etc., until at last he got to the spring to ask for water, and the spring asked for prayersticks which should pay the gods for rain. It came and he retraced his steps and was healed. The story is easily a better story than its original; it has been thoroughly adapted to its new cultural setting by the incorporation of all sorts of observations of Zuñi life, motivation has been skillfully built up, and well-known Zuñi incidents have been appropriately introduced in a thoroughly workmanlike manner.

The second ideal of the Zuñi stylist is the building up of plot sequences out of large numbers of incidents. A Zuñi audience likes very long tales, and the majority of stories combine in different ways several well-marked incidents. These incidents are stock property, and their outlines are known to all the audience. It is impossible to understand Zuñi stylistic problems without this realization of what is traditional material. The collections of Zuñi folklore that are now available do not reproduce all the tales that are told or may be told, but they give at least the elements out of which these would be built up. The study of the different variants indicates the principles of composition, and the way in which these elements, and new ones when they are introduced, are handled by the native narrators.

The principal themes in the service of which these incidents are combined have been discussed above. The narrator's skill is shown in his use of these stock incidents in elaborating these stock themes, and an examination of the tales shows clearly that this is no mean role. The way in which incidents are combined is certainly a main interest of the Zuñi audience, and the skill with which this is done by the narrator can be illustrated over and over again.

Certain of these combinations of incidents are very stable, and such complex stories as the *Box Boat* and the *Sun's Twins* follow the same sequence in Cushing's versions and in the present collection. Cushing's tales were recorded fifty years ago, and from families with quite different ceremonial affiliations and clan relationships. The sequences of incidents in these cases had very likely become popular and fairly fixed long before Cushing's time, and they may well hold firm until folktales are no longer told in Zuñi.

Even in such a tale as the *Sun's Twins*, however, the scope of the narrator in building plot is clearly marked. Version A in this collection reproduces the Cushing tale; it is the theme of the proud maiden magically impregnated by a supernatural, publicly killed because she was about to bear illegitimate children, and vindicated by her two sons at the direction of their supernatural father. The great contrast between these two versions is the cleverness with which the thoroughly non-Southwestern ceremony of the Cushing version (this part of Cushing's story has many Shoshonean analogues) has been transformed into the familiar ceremony of the Zuñi scalp dance in the present tale. This present version, moreover, has dropped the concluding incidents of the Cushing tale. This omission of the concluding incidents consolidates the plot, just as the changes in the ceremony bring it into agreement with Zuñi cultural behavior. The difference between these two versions, however, and versions B and C in this collection is more drastic. The same incidents have been used in these latter versions to elaborate a different theme: that of the sons' humiliation of the mother who abandoned them at birth. This role of the Zuñi narrator in adapting incidents to different themes is apparent in many tales. The narrator must follow out the implications of the new sequence he has chosen.

The freedom with which plots may be built up is made clear also by a consideration of certain incidents which serve as stock introductions or conclusions to a variety of tales. Whenever the plot allows its use, the incident of *Supernaturals are sent to shrines* may be called in requisition. The *Orpheus* incident is popular in a similar capacity, as well as the *Contests to retain a wife* and *Witch contests*. The *Apparition impersonated to punish evildoers or enemies* is used both as introduction and conclusion to several tales. The *Kachinas at Kachina Village provide food or clothing* is requisitioned in almost any tale in which it is appropriate. The *Marriage taught by supernaturals to those who refuse it*, the *Magical impregnations* by Sun or Horned Serpent, the *Famine is caused by misuse of corn in a game* are popular introductions to tales the plots of which differ completely.

It is obvious that where such freedom in handling incidents is expected of a good storyteller, it will often become impossible to trace with assurance a tale's genetic relationship with tales of other peoples.

The Zuñi narrator is also allowed freedom in the use of stock folkloristic devices. The loads made magically light, the runners who carry straws or gourds or feathers to run lightly, the inexhaustible meals provided by helpful animals, the magically surmounted precipices, are all legion. Good storytellers usually incorporate these devices at any appropriate point.

The greatest freedom allowed the Zuñi narrator, however, is in the adaptation of the tale to explanations and origins. Such "that's whys" are a stylistic requirement in Zuñi, and no American Indian folklore presents such a prodigality of explanatory elements. They are seldom standardized, so that the same explanatory elements occur in different versions even of the same tale, and good storytellers often give several to one tale.

The most striking way in which the importance of personal bias and experience is shown in Zuñi tales is in the contrast between tales told by men and by women. There is no taboo in Zuñi which restricts such choice. The differences that exist are the result of unconscious preference on the part of narrators. Men tell the tales which feature extended accounts of the stick races, of gambling, and of hunting. Women tell those which detail cooking techniques.[8] The Cinderella story is told by a woman, and the stories of women assisting in childbirth who discover that the mother has initiated her baby as a witch. Women also tell the only tales of poor little girls who are overworked. "Every day the little girl worked all day long. Her mother said to her, 'There is no water. Go fetch a jar of water.' The little girl cried, she was so tired she could not go for water." A moth takes pity on her and her mother grieves. Even when the little girl is brought back she cannot restrain her tears and so loses her again. The kind of detail that distinguishes the women's stories is characteristic; women give the only account of childbirth observances; women add to a description of a picnic, "The mothers nursed their babies and laid them down comfortably"; to an account of girls grinding for the priests, "Their sweethearts waited to see in which houses the girls were grinding. They drew their shawls over their faces and went in to husk for them." The one case of a mother's regret in abandoning her child at birth and her care of it is in a tale told by a woman. When the baby was born she picked it up. "She liked that baby, but she was ashamed to take it home. She broke the soft leaves off the weeds and made a nest to put it in. She broke the weeds and branches and made a shelter over the baby. She nursed it," and returned next day to renew the shelter and nurse the child again. "The third day his mother went out in the evening to see if the baby was still there. He was gone. She saw the deer tracks. She was sorry."

In two cases tales are told from the point of view of the men actors or of the women according to the sex of the narrator. The version of *The Deserted Husband* told by a woman expatiates on the woman's grievance; her husband did not compliment her on her cooking, "He never said, 'How good!'" It details the wife's determination to cook at other people's feasts and arrange a meeting with a man; it tells how she made herself beautiful, and how she went home to look after her little daughter; "She was making dolls out of rags." It follows through her arrangements with her lover and her handling of her suspicious husband. The men's versions omit all this; they tell the story from the point of view of the man.

[8] See, however, in tales told by men the bride's teaching cooking to the Ahaiyute grandmother and the good corncakes Lazy Bones makes. These are less elaborate.

They begin with the husband's proposal to bring calamity upon the pueblo because of his faithless wife, and relate the details of the kiva conversations, the ritual which causes the earthquake, the friend who informs on him, and the help of the Hopi priests.

In the *Rabbit Huntress*, the woman's version tells how the resourceful girl gets more than a man's good catch in her hunting and expends itself in an account of the making of the sand bed and presentation of the child and role of the father's mother in the birth of the child of her marriage with Ahaiyute. The man's version tells how the girl had no success in hunting and gets only two rabbits; instead of the women's details of the other version, it goes on to describe a second marriage to a human husband and how the latter followed her to the land of the dead.

One minor point remains for discussion in connection with the Zuñi tales, and that is in regard to their accuracy as history. The historical reconstructions of early ethnological students in Zuñi and Hopi were based in large measure upon the statements in folklore. Thus Fewkes interpreted the history of the Hopi as a gathering of diverse groups, now represented by the clans, from the four points of the compass; he interpreted their social organization as a consequence of these originally distinct groups. Cushing similarly, though less insistently, interpreted Zuñi migration legends. The comparison of the different versions makes it clear that the often-repeated migration incident, the *Choice of eggs*, is told with almost as many "that's whys" as any other Zuñi tale and that these explanatory elements are strictly comparable to those in courtship or witch tales. They certainly give no basis for reconstruction of history. In other examples of "that's whys" that have historic reference, the same truth is obvious. Thus the tale of *Tupe kills the Apaches* is given as the origin of the scalp dance, an origin accounted for by half a dozen other tales, and recounts a scalp dance said to have been held two generations before the tale was told to me. Obviously the scalp dance in Zuñi has no such recent origin, and the narrator himself scouted the suggestion. His "origin" was a literary flourish. In the same way a true story of treachery against Navaho visitors which happened two generations ago is told by the grandson of the chief actor as an origin of albinos in Zuñi, yet immediately after telling the tale he named albinos who had been born considerably before the date of the incident. I did not point out to him the inconsistency and he saw none. The tale did not even represent history according to his own personal knowledge.

The lack of historicity in the tales is apparent in other ways than in the explanatory elements. In the albino story a comparison with the historical account of the incident recorded by Dr. Bunzel shows that even in so short a time the tale has been built up to a climax with repetitive incidents and otherwise modified. The story of the battle which took place on Corn Mountain, at which time a friendship pact was made with the Lagunas and the Big Shell cult vanquished the enemy, is told in two historical settings, once as the tale of a quarrel with the eastern pueblos, and the other, the catastrophe of the Rebellion against the Spaniards in 1670. To the latter tale is added the story of the Spanish priest who saved the people and who elected to stay in Zuñi rather than return to his own people. It is obvious that standard literary versions of battles may do service in different connections, and that it is impossible to trust their historical accuracy.

Primitive Freedom

✤ In the 1890's, when Siberia meant to most people only a place to which Czarist Russia sent its political exiles, some of these more enterprising exiles lightened their boredom there by going native. They learned the languages of strange tribes herding mares or reindeer on the frozen tundras, traveled with them from camp to camp, and were taught by the native shamans their mediumistic lore. The most gifted of these involuntary anthropologists was Vladimïr Bogoras, who wrote Russian novels under the name of Tan. His careful account of life among the Chukchee of northeast Siberia is one of the great anthropological volumes.

He was fascinated by his rich, murderous, suiciding Chukchee. Even their routine exchanges of commodities were occasions for knifing. Their language had no word for trading; realistically enough, they called it blood-feuding. Knifing came closer home, too; sons killed their fathers,

Reprinted with permission from *The Atlantic Monthly* 169:756–63 (1942).

and brothers their brothers. And with impunity. A strong man was one who could abuse anyone, relative or stranger; and the strong man had his own way and was envied. The father's boast when a child was born was: "Ah! I have created a strong man for times to come, one who will take the property of all those living in the country around us."

Bogoras was not unfamiliar with abuses visited on one man by another; he had been exiled for protesting against them in his own country. But in Czarist Russia his protests had been directed against the state and its bene-ficiaries; to protest against abuses meant to protest against the state. And his Chukchee had no state at all. There was no political organization. Whatever men had the strength and means to do they could do. They were rich, too, beyond the dreams of all neighboring tribes. One man might own as many as three thousand reindeer, and that was great wealth. The Chukchee were, therefore, rich and democratic. If a people have no tyrannous state and if they have an abundance economy, ought they not by these circumstances to be free men? Ought they not to feel they were able to pursue and attain their own personal goals?

Nothing was clearer than that the Chukchee knew they were not free. Their word for it was "doom." They were, they said, "doomed to anger," "doomed to death," "doomed to receiving supernatural power." They spoke truly. Anger swept over them like a flood from outside themselves; they showed their teeth, they growled, they lost consciousness of what they were doing. Men—and women too—disappointed in sharing the tag-end of a smoke had killed to get hold of the pipe, and many more had ruined themselves financially because the trader had known they would stop at no price to obtain tobacco without delay. Sons, too, were "doomed" to anger against their fathers, and fathers against their sons. If they killed in their anger, it was nobody's business, and the survivors di-vided the spoils. They chose to bring about their own death, too. When they suffered from despondency or from physical pain, they preferred, they said, to destroy the self with the suffering. "We are surrounded," they said, "by enemies with gaping mouths [the spirits]," and the worst possi-ble death was the torture these gods were waiting to visit upon them; they preferred to die at their own will. When they ate the fly agaric, a poi-sonous mushroom for which they had an inordinate passion, they said to it, "Take me to the dead," and some indeed died in the coma the drug induced. Sought death was commoner, though, with a spear thrust. Young men had to rip their own bowels, but older men could vow their own death and require their sons to drive home the spear. It was a solemn duty, for a man who had once announced his wish to die a voluntary death could not take back his vow without disasters striking the whole community.

This picture of Chukchee behavior was not all that Bogoras recorded. He described also the arrangements of their social order. They lived in small encampments which had to be moved as the herd moved. The master of the herd lived in the front tent, and his ownership of the herd meant that he could dispose of all food and skins at his own will; if he chose to put his family on starvation diet, it was his prerogative. His sons or sons-in-law in the camp approached him each morning for his instructions, and he had naked power over them. Even when he became senile he could do with his family as he wished, for they all depended upon the herd. If he was bad tempered and tyrannous, the only way in which they could govern their own lives was to seize wealth and power for themselves—perhaps by killing their father.

At all events sons did not expect benefits from their fathers or from any elders. When they were no taller than their small reindeer, they were herding on the tundra, and if the half-wild animals broke away from them they were responsible like any man. After adolescence they had to obtain a wife, but this meant they had to go empty-handed like any propertyless Chukchee and serve for her. They were systematically humiliated by their prospective fathers-in-law. They slept outside the sleeping tent in the arctic weather and were fed with scraps. They were the butt of the new family's jibes and tyrannies, and if they gave up and returned home their own fathers would receive them with taunts and they had to begin service all over again in another family which had a marriageable daughter. Neither in the matter of getting a wife nor at any other time did a man have any reason to believe that his own family would assist him. If his own family did not, certainly no one else would. If a man lost his reindeer he might become a homeless wanderer, trudging from camp to camp and fed grudgingly with scraps for a day or two before he set out again on his endless tramping.

The Chukchee are a tribe with wealth and with no political autocracy, who made of life a snatch-as-snatch-can. It was not possible to live at peace and without the interference of others. They live, of course, in a punishing environment, but plenty of other preliterate people who live in earthly paradises are as "doomed" as the Chukchee. In such tribes men would laugh at you if you tried to show them that living well and at peace was really a very simple matter because the coconut and the breadfruit tree and the sago grow luxuriantly without human labor. They know that there is no open course toward well-being spread before them to follow at their own will. They know they are not free. They are conscious first and foremost of obstacles in the way of attaining their own purposes. In such societies men are intensely aware that every step toward any goal they have set themselves is at the mercy of others. They are balked at every turn, or else they win through by overpowering others. They know that, whatever they want to do, they must get the better of someone else in the community or they must play the sycophant. They know no other roles than those of aggression and of obsequiousness.

II

A couple of years ago I lived with the Blackfoot Indians of Canada. They too had been rich and they had been democratic, but in addition they were sure they had been free. Even today they could not understand the meaning of being "doomed." They were sure every man had his own personal desires and spent his life realizing them. What else would be a reason for living? Even today, when the buffalo they lived on are gone from the plains, I thought them a people to whom an understanding of liberty was as natural as breathing. How had they achieved a way of life that was so opposite to the Chukchee?

They were full of tales of their great chief Eagle in the Skies, and many early settlers and travelers had also written about him. Eagle in the Skies was chief of an illustrious Blackfoot band and he was rich. All the Blackfoot cared about wealth, and they thought that people without wealth were inferior. Eagle in the Skies was a superior being and he had wealth to prove it. He had been a great hunter and raider of horses. He could provide for a whole coterie of wives who dressed skins for him, made beaded skin garments, dried meat, and made pemmican. As the most successful provider in the band, he was made chief. But a chief among

137

the Blackfoot was not invested with punitive power over his people, and his prestige depended on his band's prestige.

His followers' personal ambitions were Eagle's greatest assets, and it was against his interests to balk them. A young retainer, as yet un-mounted, had only to be known as a good horseman to be free to use Eagle's horses in hunting or on a raid. What the young man took contrib-uted to the glory and well-being of Eagle's band, but kudos belonged to the young hunter, even the kudos of distributing the horses or the buffalo meat. The indigent young man's family boasted of his prowess, parading the camp circle and shouting his achievements. The young man himself began looking for a wife among the daughters of leading men who would be glad of such a son-in-law. Without the use of Eagle's horses he would not have been able to make his mark in the tribe's esti-mation, but such use was no charity; whether the young man brought in buffalo or the enemy's horses, it enlarged Eagle's ego no less than the young hunter's. It was strictly to Eagle's advantage to have a well-fed and well-mounted band. Blackfoot in other bands, dissatisfied with the leaders in their own communities, took occasion to join Eagle's and share in its prosperity. Eagle's band grew. He was well served and so were his followers. When a poor young man lost one of Eagle's good horses on a raid, the chief wrote it off. What was an occasional horse to him when sharing with his followers brought him such large returns? Mutual advantage flowed between the chief and his adherents.

Eagle in the Skies served his own ends by seeing that his people could rise according to their abilities. He served their ends also. Any of his followers, if he had ability, could reach any position in the tribe. If he underwent the training and paid the price, he could have supernatural power. His father-in-law was a principal benefactor throughout his life, and he in turn distributed to his father-in-law a principal part of his take either in hunting or on the warpath. At any step in his career, if he had earned their respect, he could be sure of the praise and active support of his fellows in his undertakings.

There are many such tribes. In these societies the higher a man climbs in status the more responsibilities he must shoulder for his fellows. What else could status mean according to their way of thinking? When any man, on the contrary, is out of luck, it is no catastrophe. Someone with whom he divided his kangaroo meat over and over again, when he brought in game, shares with him as a matter of course. It is tribal custom. When he grows too feeble to be an active hunter, his son-in-law brings him the best cuts just as the old man when he was younger took his best cuts to his own father-in-law. Much of his behavior seems to us to put the interests of others above his own interests, but he would be completely incredulous if you tried to point this out to him. It appears to him that he has always done as he chose to do. Why else did he live?

III

We need to inquire from such societies as these what it is that makes for well-being and a sense of freedom in tribes like the Blackfoot and for the conviction of doom in tribes like the Chukchee. We are fighting today a war which is to preserve freedom, and we need to know its proved strategy. We need a wider range of cases than are available to us from the troubled democracies of our day, and for these we can best go to the anthropologist.

The anthropologist has many instances spread before him, for he studies human societies as different as possible from our own, and specializes in simple societies which have grown up outside the sphere of influence of Western civilization. He can study the strategy by which societies have realized one or another set of values, whether these values have to do with freedom or social cohesion or submission to authority. His tribes serve him as a laboratory serves when we investigate, for instance, the life and death of bacteria. To be sure, the anthropological laboratory is not one the investigator sets up himself; it was set up for him by generations of natives working out their own way of life in all its details over many thousands of years. But the field worker has only to study his own particular tribe to recognize, even if it is in an unfamiliar guise, most of our current issues.

His naked savages do not, of course, talk of social security acts, but they are entirely explicit about the care of the old and the hungry. Some tribes take care of them and some do not, and the anthropologist can study the consequences. Nor do his natives speak of a golden rule, but the working of the golden rule can be studied among natives from Australia to the Kalahari Desert. "Who will feed you if you do not feed them?";

"Who will honor you if you do not honor them?" are themes which are dinned into the young and lived out in detail by adults in native South Sea Islands and under the cold fogs of Tierra del Fuego. There are equally primitive tribes which have no version at all of the golden rule, and the anthropologist can study the consequences of its absence just as well as of its presence. Is it power over people? Some primitive peoples hardly know any other way of handling human relations, and some, on the other hand, have never had occasion arbitrarily to coerce another human being.

So too with liberty. Liberty is the battle standard we fight under today, but we are at odds about the strategy of attaining it. The issue which is relevant to liberty is now, as it has always been, what societies do about the individual's pursuit of his own goals; and some societies are as successful as the Blackfoot in rearing men convinced of their freedom, and some are as unsuccessful as the Chukchee.

The first question we need to ask about such societies is whether they are free because they are democracies. Even a preliterate tribe is democratic if there is no entrenched political autocracy and if social control is ultimately in the hands of citizens. But being a democracy has not by itself guaranteed the blessings of liberty. In many democracies men do not sleep well nights in the confidence that they are safe from the aggressions of the fellow tribesmen. This is unfortunate for them, for their lives become full of violence and frustration, but it is fortunate for us because from their experience we can get information we desperately need.

The mere fact of leaving ultimate social control in the hands of the people has not guaranteed that men will be able to conduct their lives as free men. Those societies where men know they are free are often democracies, but sometimes they have strong chiefs and kings. Whether they are democracies or kingdoms, they have, however, one common characteristic: they are all alike in making certain freedoms common to all citizens, and inalienable. In our American vocabulary all those things which from time to time society has put beyond the reach of arbitrary interference by other men we call civil liberties. Habeas corpus, equality before the law, freedom of opinion and of assembly, stand or fall according as they are guaranteed to all men. They stand or fall according as it is true that what privilege I have, you have too. Civil liberties are only privileges which men in some societies have agreed to make common property for all citizens.

So too in primitive societies there are civil liberties, the crux of which is that they are guaranteed to all men without discrimination. Wherever these privileges and protections to which all members have an inalienable right are important privileges in the eyes of that tribe, people regard themselves, whatever their form of government, as free men enjoying the blessings of liberty.

IV

Every society has a different list of these civil liberties. Some are longer than ours, some are shorter and more restricted. Some are guaranteed by formal law and some are upheld simply by the folkways. The one that is commonest in human societies is the right to hospitality. Any man sets food before his guest, often even without questioning whether or not he is a tribesman. But as a civil liberty within the tribe it goes much farther than days-long hospitality. As in the Blackfoot camp of Chief Eagle in the Skies, no man goes hungry while there is food in the community, and he exercises this right to subsistence not as a claim on charity but as a civil liberty which all tribesmen share. In any season of scarcity, for example, it does not matter who brings in the game or who owns the grain or the herds: the meals are served to all in common, share and share alike, or else through the etiquette of hospitality all those whose supplies are low are guests of those who are well provided. There will be "turn about" someday.

In some tribes, eating from each other's pots becomes a symbol whose value has nothing to do with utility; it becomes obsessive. When the pots boil in the evening before each house, women dish up the food and carry it hither and yon to other houses, receiving in turn the stew from all their neighbors. Each family gathers at last around a pot which contains the cooking of a couple of dozen housewives. There is no measuring of *quid pro quo;* they have elaborated the common and inalienable right to an evening meal till it means to them that all villagers should eat the contents of all pots.

Another civil liberty that is common among native tribes is one which is guaranteed the young when they become physically able to earn their own livelihood. Such tribes regard it as a tribal good that all boys and girls, as soon as they have sufficient strength to do the work of adults, should be provided with tools and fields and herds so that they can contribute to the community food supply. This would often be impossible if they were dependent solely on their parents, and different primitive societies have different ways of solving this youth problem.

Many South American Indian villages which depended on their corn fields for their food had annual reallotments of fields so that each able-bodied man might be responsible for tending the acreage he could actually cultivate. Some tribes in other parts of the world pay youngsters with disproportionate gifts during their apprentice period, so that anyone who is not congenitally lazy can count on having an adult's equipment by the time he is ready to take on a man's responsibility.

In other tribes skills are far more important than the tools of production, and especially in hunting tribes the stress is all upon building up the boy's ability and self-confidence in the exercise of daring feats in tracking the bear or bringing down the buffalo. The child's ability is carefully reckoned against his past achievement, not against some arbitrary or adult standard; he is shown how to hunt by a much older brother or by an uncle, and he is encouraged by village-wide praise when he has taken the initiative and brought in even a tiny rodent. With each larger animal he bags he is again acclaimed. It would be foolish, they think, not to build up a child's self-confidence.

One of the most impotant of civil liberties in such tribes is the opportunity to enter any profession according to a man's individual ability. When status is thus open and can be freely achieved, any man can weigh the responsibility of important status against its prerogatives and limit his ambitions accordingly. He often accepts gladly the role of follower even though chieftainship has its obvious glamour. A great deal is required of the chief, and many men are willing enough to play a lesser part. A great deal is required of the rich man and the shaman and the priest, of the war leader and the owner of many medicine bundles. Many men choose not to undertake the rigorousness of the training or the responsibilities of the position.

V

When, however, a privileged group can act arbitrarily and without responsibility and still retain its privileges, men's individual goals are threatened. This is not because one group has great prerogatives, for Eagle in the Skies had his great prerogatives too. It is because, as among the Chukchee, these are split off from responsibility and respect for those upon whose labor the advantages depend; it is because under that particular social order men can keep personal advantages without returning equivalents. Then freedom is threatened.

Freedom in all societies therefore must have this ingredient of the exchange of equivalents. Privilege must mean more equivalents returned rather than less. If the king has emoluments, he must be able to use them only so that his people feel he acts for them. If a medicine man has supernatural power, he must not be able to use it to kill others by lingering death, but his prayers must provide rain for the fields, and increase and long life for the people. If the rich are privileged, their possessions must not disallow the subsistence of others or preëmpt natural resources. Otherwise men do not feel confident about their personal goals. They know they are not free of hindrance, and they act with all the furtiveness and the aggression that goes along with serious frustration. They are not free men—not even the privileged. For in societies where advantages can be achieved only at the expense of others, the great and powerful are, if possible, even more vulnerable than the weak. They can never reach a security that cannot be cut at its roots, and "the tallest oak has the greatest fall."

Societies which make privilege inseparable from trusteeship have been able to perpetuate and extend civil liberties. They have been able to unite the whole society into a kind of joint-stock company where any denial of rights is a threat to each and every member. It is the basis upon which strong and zestful societies are built and the basis for the individual's sense of inner freedom.

This analysis of freedom does not sound so alien in Western civilization in times of war as it does in times of peace. War is the one situation in our society when we rally for mutual advantage and call on every man to show group loyalty. It is ironic that nations which exalt personal profit as the one way in which to keep the wheels of industry moving should in wartime eradicate or conceal the profit motive and trust again in group loyalty. In this major emergency we turn away from the competitive motive. In spite of all the declarations of learned writers that working for profit is the only incentive upon which society can depend, in war we know it is too weak and too expensive. We invoke again cooperation for the common good and the defense of our country. And it is a commonplace that men like war. For peace, in our society, with the feeling we have then that it is feeble-minded to strive except for one's own private profit, is a lonely thing and a hazardous business. Over and over men have proved that they prefer the hazards of war with all its suffering. It has its compensations.

The moral is not that war is therefore an inevitable human need, but that our social order starves men in peacetime for gratifications they get only in time of war. Many Indians of the great Mississippi plains, on the other hand, set up war and peace in reverse. Their peacetime dealings with their fellow tribesmen were arranged in joint-stock-company fashion with pooled profits and limited liability. Their primitive guerrilla warfare, however, was a field in which private advantage could be safely sought at the expense of an enemy they did not even count as "human." The Dakota Indians were brave and inveterate followers of the warpath. They were feared by all neighboring tribes. But the state had no stake in their exploits; no armies were sent out for political objectives, and the idea of establishing their sovereignty over another tribe had not occurred to them. Young men on the warpath accumulated long lists of standardized exploits—for getting away with an enemy's horse picketed in his camp circle, for touching a fallen enemy who was still alive, for taking a scalp, for bringing a slain or wounded tribesman from the enemy's lines, for having a horse shot under one. These coups, as the voyagers called them, they totaled up and used for vying with their fellows. The warpath and all that went with it was competitive. A man joined a war party for no reasons of patriotism, but because he wanted to make his mark. When the party got to enemy country, each man put on his finest regalia and the feather headdress, each feather of which was insignia of a coup he had previously taken. When the party returned to its home camp, those who had coups to their credit were extravagantly acclaimed by all those families who could in any way claim relationship to the heroes. To their dying day warriors boasted competitively of their accumulated coups. A hundred or more counting sticks were kept in the council house, and men "won" who had the right to take up the greatest number of sticks and tell their exploits.

Life within the Dakota tribe, on the other hand, and all dealings within the community, rested solidly on mutual advantage and group loyalty. The large family connections, the band, even the whole tribe, was a cooperating group where mutual support brought every man honor. The worst thing that could be said of a Dakota was: "He thinks more of what he owns than he does of people." They took it literally and in great giveaways they showed how much they "cared for people"; obviously, too, giving lavishly raised the giver's own standing in the tribe. *Noblesse oblige* they took literally too. A person who had risen high and who had a strong and prosperous family must be by that token the most generous and the most willing to give all kinds of assistance. It was an essential part of his honorable status. The Dakota had tied group loyalty inextricably to times of peace.

The war against the Axis in 1942 is not Dakota guerrilla warfare which each man can fight out by himself to gain his own personal coup. It is a war between two ideologies about the way to set up human societies. Nazi theory and practice have abjured the strategy of freedom and oppose to it submission to a leader and individual sacrifice to a New Order in which lesser breeds are to be slaves and servitors to the fittest and dominant conquerors. The democracies, with all their shortcomings, base their philosophy upon freedoms which *can* be made common and provide political frameworks which can be used to extend them. Axis oratory uses the word "freedom," but Axis "freedoms" are those which *cannot* be made common, because they imply an underdog. They are the "freedoms" to expropriate from a subject people, to use naked force against the helpless, to drag dissenters from their homes and kill them out of hand. The Axis has made these measures the tools of state administration, and these measures cut civil liberties at their roots. The nation which rules others by terror must extend its reign of terror. It must continue to follow the path it has chosen.

There is solid reason, therefore, in the history of human societies, for the opposition of the democracies to the spread of the Nazi state and of Nazi ideology. But this solid reason is grounded on the social utility of civil liberties, the liberties which can be made common property. Civil liberties in all human societies have always paid their way; they have given advantages to all citizens and all tribesmen. Special privileges, arbitrary power, on the other hand, are boomerangs which return to strike those who wield them, and they bring conflict and often terror into the whole society. Therefore, we in America are willing to pay enormous prices lest liberty be lost on our continent. The only argument is how best to keep ourselves strong and uncontaminated. For this great end we must be clear in our minds that the way to keep ourselves from the taint of our enemies is through the defense of civil liberties. We must be sure that we do not curtail them in the fields already allowed, and we must extend them to other fields not now recognized. For liberty is the one thing no man can have unless he grants it to others.

Self-Discipline in Japanese Culture

✤ The self-disciplines of one culture are always likely to seem irrelevancies to observers from another country. The disciplinary techniques themselves are clear enough, but why go to all the trouble? Why voluntarily hang yourself from hooks, or concentrate on your navel, or never spend your capital? Why concentrate on one of these austerities and demand no control at all over some impulses which to the outsider are truly important and in need of training? When the observer belongs to a country which does not teach technical methods of self-discipline and is set down in the midst of a people who place great reliance upon them, the possibility of misunderstanding is at its height.

In the United States technical and traditional methods of self-discipline are relatively undeveloped. The American assumption is that a man, having sized up what is possible in his personal life, will discipline himself, if that is necessary, to attain a chosen goal. Whether he does or not, de-

REPRINTED WITH PERMISSION of Houghton Mifflin Company from *The Chrysanthemum and the Sword: Patterns of Japanese Culture* (1946), pp. 228–52 (abridged).

pends on his ambition, or his conscience, or his 'instinct of work-manship,' as Veblen called it. He may accept a Stoic regime in order to play on a football team, or give up all relaxations to train himself as a musician, or to make a success of his business. He may eschew evil and frivolity because of his conscience. But in the United States self-discipline itself, as a technical training, is not a thing to learn like arithmetic quite apart from its application in a particular instance. . . .

The Japanese assumption, however, is that a boy taking his middle-school examinations, or a man playing in a fencing match, or a person merely living the life of an aristocrat, needs a self-training quite apart from learning the specific things that will be required of him when he is tested. No matter what facts he has crammed for his examination, no matter how expert his sword thrusts, no matter how meticulous his punc-tilio, he needs to lay aside his books and his sword and his public appear-ances and undergo a special kind of training. Not all Japanese submit to esoteric training, of course, but, even for those who do not, the phraseol-ogy and the practice of self-discipline have a recognized place in life. Jap-anese of all classes judge themselves and others in terms of a whole set of concepts which depend upon their notion of generalized technical self-control and self-governance.

Their concepts of self-discipline can be schematically divided into those which give competence and those which give something more. This something more I shall call expertness. The two are divided in Japan and aim at accomplishing a different result in the human psyche and have a different rationale and are recognized by different signs. . . .

Americans, in order to understand ordinary self-disciplinary practices in Japan, have to do a kind of surgical operation on our idea of 'self-dis-cipline.' We have to cut away the accretions of 'self-sacrifice' and 'frustra-tion' that have clustered around the concept in our culture. In Japan one disciplines oneself to be a good player, and the Japanese attitude is that one undergoes the training with no more consciousness of sacrifice than a man who plays bridge. Of course the training is strict, but that is inherent in the nature of things. The young child is born happy but without the capacity to 'savor life.' Only through mental training (or self-discipline; *shuyo*) can a man or woman gain the power to live fully and to 'get the taste' of life. The phrase is usually translated 'only so can he enjoy life.'

Self-discipline 'builds up the belly (the seat of control)'; it enlarges life.

'Competent' self-discipline in Japan has this rationale that it improves a man's conduct of his own life. Any impatience he may feel while he is new in the training will pass, they say, for eventually he will enjoy it—or give it up. An apprentice tends properly to his business, a boy learns *judo* (jujitsu), a young wife adjusts to the demands of her mother-in-law; it is quite understood that in the first stages of training, the man or woman unused to the new requirements may wish to be free of this shuyo. Their fathers may talk to them and say, 'What do you wish? Some training is necessary to savor life. If you give this up and do not train yourself at all, you will be unhappy as a natural consequence. And if these natural consequences should occur, I should not be inclined to protect you against public opinion.' Shuyo, in the phrase they use so often, polishes away 'the rust of the body.' It makes a man a bright sharp sword, which is, of course, what he desires to be.

All this stress on how self-discipline leads to one's own advantage does not mean that the extreme acts the Japanese code often requires are not truly serious frustrations, and that such frustrations do not lead to aggressive impulses. This distinction is one which Americans understand in games and sports. The bridge champion does not complain of the self-sacrifice that has been required of him to learn to play well; he does not label as 'frustrations' the hours he has had to put in in order to become an expert. Nevertheless, physicians say that in some cases the great attention necessary when a man is playing either for high stakes or for a championship, is not unrelated to stomach ulcers and excessive bodily tensions. The same thing happens to people in Japan. But the sanction of reciprocity, and the Japanese conviction that self-discipline is to one's own advantage, make many acts seem easy to them which seem insupportable to Americans. They pay much closer attention to behaving competently and they allow themselves fewer alibis than Americans. They do not so often project their dissatisfactions with life upon scapegoats, and they do not so often indulge in self-pity because they have somehow or other not got what Americans call average happiness. They have been trained to pay much closer attention to the 'rust of the body' than is common among Americans.

Beyond and above 'competent' self-discipline, there is also the plane of 'expertness.' Japanese techniques of this latter sort have not been made very intelligible to Western readers by Japanese authors who have written about them, and Occidental scholars who have made a specialty of this subject have often been very cavalier about them. Sometimes they have called them 'eccentricities.' One French scholar writes that they are all 'in defiance of common sense,' and that the greatest of all disciplinary sects, the Zen cult, is 'a tissue of solemn nonsense.' The purposes their techniques are intended to accomplish, however, are not impenetrable, and the whole subject throws a considerable light on Japanese psychic economy.

A long series of Japanese words name the state of mind the expert in self-discipline is supposed to achieve. Some of these terms are used for actors, some for religious devotees, some for fencers, some for public speakers, some for painters, some for masters of the tea ceremony. They all have the same general meaning, and I shall use only the word *muga*, which is the word used in the flourishing upper-class cult of Zen Buddhism. The description of this state of expertness is that it denotes those experiences, whether secular or religious, when 'there is no break, not even the thickness of a hair' between a man's will and his act. A discharge of electricity passes directly from the positive to the negative pole. In people who have not attained expertness, there is, as it were, a nonconducting screen which stands between the will and the act. They call this the 'observing self,' the 'interfering self,' and when this has been removed by special kinds of training the expert loses all sense that 'I am doing it.' The circuit runs free. The act is effortless. It is 'one-pointed.' The deed completely reproduces the picture the actor had drawn of it in his mind. . . .

Many civilizations have developed techniques of this kind, but the Japanese goals and methods have a marked character all their own. This is especially interesting because many of the techniques are derived from India where they are known as Yoga. Japanese techniques of self-hypnotism, concentration, and control of the senses still show kinship with Indian practices. There is similar emphasis on emptying the mind, on immobility of the body, on ten thousands of repetitions of the same phrase, on fixing the attention on a chosen symbol. Even the terminology used in India is still recognizable. Beyond these bare bones of the

149

cult, however, the Japanese version has little in common with the Hindu.

Yoga in India is an extreme cult of asceticism. It is a way of obtaining release from the round of reincarnation. Man has no salvation except this release, *nirvana*, and the obstacle in his path is human desire. These desires can be eliminated by starving them out, by insulting them, and by courting self-torture. Through these means a man may reach sainthood and achieve spirituality and union with the divine. Yoga is a way of renouncing the world of the flesh and of escaping the treadmill of human futility. It is also a way of laying hold of spiritual powers. The journey toward one's goal is the faster the more extreme the asceticism.

Such philosophy is alien in Japan. Even though Japan is a great Buddhist nation, ideas of transmigration and of nirvana have never been a part of the Buddhist faith of the people. These doctrines are personally accepted by some Buddhist priests, but they have never affected folkways or popular thought. No animal or insect is spared in Japan because killing it would kill a transmigrated human soul, and Japanese funeral ceremonies and birth rituals are innocent of any notions of a round of reincarnations. Transmigration is not a Japanese pattern of thought. The idea of nirvana, too, not only means nothing to the general public but the priesthoods themselves modify it out of existence. Priestly scholars declare that a man who has been 'enlightened' (*satori*) is already in nirvana; nirvana is here and now in the midst of time, and a man 'sees nirvana' in a pine tree and a wild bird. The Japanese have always been uninterested in fantasies of a world of the hereafter. Their mythology tells of gods but not of the life of the dead. They have even rejected Buddhist ideas of differential rewards and punishments after death. Any man, the least farmer, becomes a Buddha when he dies; the very word for the family memorial tablets in the household shrine is 'the Buddhas.' No other Buddhist country uses such language, and when a nation speaks so boldly of its ordinary dead, it is quite understandable that it does not picture any such difficult goal as attainment of nirvana. A man who becomes a Buddha anyway need not set himself to attain the goal of absolute surcease by lifelong mortification of the flesh.

Just as alien in Japan is the doctrine that the flesh and the spirit are irreconcilable. Yoga is a technique to eliminate desire, and desire has its seat in the flesh. But the Japanese do not have this dogma. 'Human feel-ings' are not of the Evil One, and it is a part of wisdom to enjoy the pleasures of the senses. The one condition is that they be sacrificed to the serious duties of life. This tenet is carried to its logical extreme in the Jap-anese handling of the Yoga cult: not only are all self-tortures eliminated but the cult in Japan is not even one of asceticism. Even the 'Enlight-ened' in their retreats, though they were called hermits, commonly es-tablished themselves in comfort with their wives and children in charming spots in the country. The companionship of their wives and even the birth of subsequent children were regarded as entirely compatible with their sanctity. In the most popular of all Buddhist sects priests marry any-way and raise families; Japan has never found it easy to accept the theory that the spirit and the flesh are incompatible. The saintliness of the 'enlightened' consisted in their self-disciplinary meditations and in their simplification of life. It did not consist in wearing unclean clothing or shutting one's eyes to the beauties of nature or one's ears to the beauty of stringed instruments. Their saints might fill their days with the composi-tion of elegant verses, the ritual of tea ceremony and 'viewings' of the moon and the cherry blossoms. The Zen cult even directs its devotees to avoid 'the three insufficiencies: insufficiency of clothing, of food, and of sleep.'

The final tenet of Yoga philosophy is also alien in Japan: that the tech-niques of mysticism which it teaches transport the practitioner to ecstatic union with the Universe. Wherever the techniques of mysticism have been practiced in the world, whether by primitive peoples or by Moham-medan dervishes or by Indian Yogis or by medieval Christians, those who practice them have almost universally agreed, whatever their creed, that they become 'one with the divine,' that they experience ecstasy 'not of this world.' The Japanese have the techniques of mysticism without the mysticism. This does not mean that they do not achieve trance. They do. But they regard even trance as a technique which trains a man in 'one-pointedness.' They do not describe it as ecstasy. The Zen cult does not even say, as mystics in other countries do, that the five senses are in abeyance in trance; they say that the 'six' senses are brought by this tech-nique to a condition of extraordinary acuteness. The sixth sense is located in the mind, and training makes it supreme over the ordinary five, but taste, touch, sight, smell, and hearing are given their own special training during trance. It is one of the exercises of group Zen to perceive sound- less footsteps and be able to follow them accurately as they pass from one place to another or to discriminate tempting odors of food—purposely in- troduced—without breaking trance. Smelling, seeing, hearing, touching, and tasting 'help the sixth sense,' and one learns in this state to make 'every sense alert.'

This is very unusual training in any cult of extra-sensory experience. Even in trance such a Zen practitioner does not try to get outside of him- self, but in the phrase Nietzsche uses of the ancient Greeks, 'to remain what he is and retain his civic name.' There are many vivid statements of this view of the matter among the sayings of the great Japanese Buddhist teachers. One of the best is that of Dogen, the great thirteenth-century founder of the Soto cult of Zen, which is still the largest and most influ- ential of the Zen cults. Speaking of his own enlightenment (satori), he said, 'I recognized only that my eyes were horizontal above my perpen- dicular nose. . . . There is nothing mysterious (in Zen experience). Time passes as it is natural, the sun rising in the east and the moon set- ting in the west.' [1] Nor do Zen writings allow that trance experience gives power other than self-disciplined human power; 'Yoga claims that various supernatural powers can be acquired by meditation,' a Japanese Buddhist writes, 'but Zen does not make any such absurd claims.' [2]

The Japanese thus wipe the slate clean of the assumptions on which Yoga practices are based in India. Japan, with a vital love of finitude which reminds one of the ancient Greeks, understands the technical practices of Yoga as being a self-training in perfection, a means whereby a man may obtain that 'expertness' in which there is not the thickness of a hair between a man and his deed. It is a training in efficiency. It is a training in self-reliance. Its rewards are here and now, for it enables a man to meet any situation with exactly the right expenditure of effort, neither too much nor too little, and it gives him control of his otherwise wayward mind so that neither physical danger from outside nor passion from within can dislodge him.

Such training is of course just as valuable for a warrior as for a priest,

[1] Kaiten Nukariya, *The Religion of the Samurai* (London: Luzac, 1913), p. 197.
[2] *Ibid.*, p. 194.

and it was precisely the warriors of Japan who made the Zen cult their own. One can hardly find elsewhere than in Japan techniques of mysticism pursued without the reward of the consummating mystic experience and appropriated by warriors to train them for hand-to-hand combat. Yet this has been true from the earliest period of Zen influence in Japan. The great book by the Japanese founder, Ei-sai, in the twelfth century was called *The Protection of the State by the Propagation of Zen*, and Zen has trained warriors, statesmen, fencers, and university students to achieve quite mundane goals. As Sir Charles Eliot says, nothing in the history of the Zen cult in China gave any indication of the future that awaited it as a military discipline in Japan. 'Zen has become as decidedly Japanese as tea ceremonies or Noh plays. It might have been supposed that in a troubled period like the twelfth and thirteenth centuries this contemplative and mystic doctrine, which finds truth not in scripture but in the immediate experience of the human mind, would have flourished in monastic harbours of refuge among those who had left the storms of the world, but not that it would have been accepted as the favourite rule of life for the military class. Yet such it became.' [3]

Many Japanese sects, both Buddhist and Shintoist, have laid great emphasis on mystic techniques of contemplation, self-hypnotism, and trance. Some of them, however, claim the result of this training as evidences of the grace of God and base their philosophy on *tariki*, 'help of another,' i.e., of a gracious god. Some of them, of which Zen is the paramount example, rely only on 'self-help', *jiriki*. The potential strength, they teach, lies only within oneself, and only by one's own efforts can one increase it. Japanese samurai found this entirely congenial, and whether as monks, statesmen, or educators—for they served in all these rôles—they used the Zen techniques to buttress a rugged individualism. Zen teachings were excessively explicit. 'Zen seeks only the light man can find in himself. It tolerates no hindrance to this seeking. Clear every obstacle out of your way. . . . If on your way you meet Buddha, kill him! If you meet the Patriarchs, kill them! If you meet the Saints, kill them all. That is the only way of reaching salvation.' [4]

[3] Sir Charles Eliot, *Japanese Buddhism* (London: Longmans, 1935), p. 186.
[4] Quoted in E. Steinilber-Oberlin and Kuni Matsuo, *The Buddhist Sects of Japan* (trans. from the French; New York: Macmillan, 1938), p. 143.

He who seeks after truth must take nothing at second-hand, no teaching of the Buddha, no scriptures, no theology. 'The twelve chapters of the Buddhist canon are a scrap of paper.' One may with profit study them, but they have nothing to do with the lightning flash in one's own soul which is all that gives Enlightenment. In a Zen book of dialogues a novice asks a Zen priest to expound the Sutra of the Lotus of the Good Law. The priest gave him a brilliant exposition, and the listener said witheringly, 'Why, I thought Zen priests disdained texts, theories, and systems of logical explanations.' 'Zen,' returned the priest, 'does not consist in knowing nothing, but in the belief that *to know* is outside of all texts, of all documents. You did not tell me you wanted *to know*, but only that you wished an explanation of the text.' [5]

The traditional training given by Zen teachers was intended to teach novices how 'to know.' The training might be physical or it might be mental, but it must be finally validated in the inner consciousness of the learner. Zen training of the fencer illustrates this well. The fencer, of course, has to learn and constantly practice the proper sword thrusts, but his proficiency in these belongs in the field of mere 'competence.' In addition he must learn to be *muga*. He is made to stand first on the level floor, concentrating on the few inches of surface which support his body. This tiny surface of standing room is gradually raised till he has learned to stand as easily on a four-foot pillar as in a court yard. When he is perfectly secure on that pillar, he 'knows.' His mind will no longer betray him by dizziness and fear of falling.

This Japanese use of pillar-standing transforms the familiar Western medieval austerity of Saint Simeon Stylites into a purposeful self-discipline. It is no longer an austerity. All kinds of physical exercises in Japan, whether of the Zen cult, or the common practices of the peasant villages, undergo this kind of transformation. In many places of the world diving into freezing water and standing under mountain waterfalls, are standard austerities, sometimes to mortify the flesh, sometimes to obtain pity from the gods, sometimes to induce trance. The favorite Japanese cold-austerity was standing or sitting in an ice-cold waterfall before dawn, or dousing oneself three times during a winter night with icy water. But the object was to train one's conscious self till one no longer noticed the

[5] *Ibid.*, p. 175.

discomfort. A devotee's purpose was to train himself to continue his meditation without interruption. When neither the cold shock of the water nor the shivering of the body in the cold dawn registered in his consciousness he was 'expert.' There was no other reward.

Mental training had to be equally self-appropriated. A man might associate himself with a teacher, but the teacher could not 'teach' in the Occidental sense, because nothing a novice learned from any source outside himself was of any importance. The teacher might hold discussions with the novice, but he did not lead him gently into a new intellectual realm. The teacher was considered to be most helpful when he was most rude. If, without warning, the master broke the tea bowl the novice was raising to his lips, or tripped him, or struck his knuckles with a brass rod, the shock might galvanize him into sudden insight. It broke through his complacency. The monkish books are filled with incidents of this kind.

The most favored technique for inducing the novice's desperate attempt 'to know' were the *koan*, literally 'the problems.' There are said to be seventeen hundred of these problems, and the anecdote books make nothing of a man's devoting seven years to the solution of one of them. They are not meant to have rational solutions. One is 'To conceive the clapping of one hand.' Another is 'To feel the yearning for one's mother before one's own conception.' Others are, 'Who is carrying one's lifeless body?' 'Who is it who is walking toward me?' 'All things return into One; where does this last return?' Such Zen problems as these were used in China before the twelfth or thirteenth century, and Japan adopted these techniques along with the cult. On the continent, however, they did not survive. In Japan they are a most important part of training in 'expertness.' Zen handbooks treat them with extreme seriousness. 'Koan enshrine the dilemma of life.' A man who is pondering one, they say, reaches an impasse like 'a pursued rat that has run up a blind tunnel,' he is like a man 'with a ball of red-hot iron stuck in his throat,' he is 'a mosquito trying to bite a lump of iron.' He is beside himself and redoubles his efforts. Finally the screen of his 'observing self' between his mind and his problem falls aside; with the swiftness of a flash of lightning the two—mind and problem—come to terms. He 'knows.'

After these descriptions of bow-string-taut mental effort it is an anticlimax to search the incident books for great truths gained with all this

155

expenditure. Nangaku, for instance, spent eight years on the problem, 'Who is it who is walking toward me?' At last he understood. His words were: 'Even when one affirms that there is something here, one omits the whole.' Nevertheless, there is a general pattern in the revelations. It is suggested in the lines of dialogue:

Novice: How shall I escape from the Wheel of Birth and Death?

Master: Who puts you under restraint? (I.e., binds you to this Wheel.) What they learn, they say, is, in the famous Chinese phrase, that they 'were looking for an ox when they were riding on one.' They learn that 'What is necessary is not the net and the trap but the fish or the animal these instruments were meant to catch.' They learn, that is, in Occidental phraseology, that both horns of the dilemma are irrelevant. They learn that goals may be attained with present means if the eyes of the spirit are opened. Anything is possible, and with no help from anyone but oneself.

The significance of the koan does not lie in the truths these seekers after truth discover, which are the world-wide truths of the mystics. It lies in the way the Japanese conceive the search for truth.

The koan are called 'bricks with which to knock upon the door.' 'The door' is in the wall built around unenlightened human nature, which worries about whether present means are sufficient and fantasies to itself a cloud of watchful witnesses who will allot praise or blame. It is the wall of *haji* (shame) which is so real to all Japanese. Once the brick has battered down the door and it has fallen open, one is in free air and one throws away the brick. One does not go on solving more koan. The lesson has been learned and the Japanese dilemma of virtue has been solved. They have thrown themselves with desperate intensity against an impasse; for 'the sake of the training' they have become as 'mosquitoes biting a lump of iron.' In the end they have learned that there is no impasse—no impasse between gimu and giri, either, or between giri and human feelings, between righteousness and giri. They have found a way out. They are free and for the first time they can fully 'taste' life. They are muga. Their training in 'expertness' has been successfully achieved.

Suzuki, the great authority on Zen Buddhism, describes muga as 'ecstasy with no sense of *I am doing it*,' 'effortlessness.' [6] The 'observing self'

[6] Daisetz Teitaro Suzuki, *Essays in Zen Buddhism*, 3 vols. (Boston: Marshall Jones, 1927–1934), 3:318.

is eliminated; a man 'loses himself,' that is, he ceases to be a spectator of his acts. Suzuki says: 'With the awaking of consciousness, the will is split into two: . . . actor and observer. Conflict is inevitable, for the actor (-self) wants to be free from the limitations' of the observer-self. Therefore in Enlightenment the disciple discovers that there is no observer-self, 'no soul entity as an unknown or unknowable quantity.' [7] Nothing remains but the goal and the act that accomplishes it. The student of human behavior could rephrase this statement to refer more particularly to Japanese culture. As a child a person is drastically trained to observe his own acts and to judge them in the light of what people will say; his observer-self is terribly vulnerable. To deliver himself up to the ecstasy of his soul, he eliminates this vulnerable self. He ceases to feel that '*he* is doing it.' He then feels himself trained in his soul in the same way that the novice in fencing feels himself trained to stand without fear of falling on the four-foot pillar.

The painter, the poet, the public speaker and the warrior use this training in muga similarly. They acquire, not Infinitude, but a clear undisturbed perception of finite beauty or adjustment of means and ends so that they can use just the right amount of effort, 'no more and no less,' to achieve their goal.

Even a person who has undergone no training at all may have a sort of muga experience. When a man watching Noh or Kabuki plays completely loses himself in the spectacle, he too is said to lose his observing self. The palms of his hands become wet. He feels 'the sweat of muga.' A bombing pilot approaching his goal has 'the sweat of muga' before he releases his bombs. '*He* is not doing it.' There is no observer-self left in his consciousness. An anti-aircraft gunner, lost to all the world beside, is said similarly to have 'the sweat of muga' and to have eliminated the observer-self. The idea is that in all such cases people in this condition are at the top of their form.

Such concepts are eloquent testimony to the heavy burden the Japanese make out of self-watchfulness and self-surveillance. They are free and efficient, they say, when these restraints are gone. Whereas Americans identify their observer-selves with the rational principle within them and pride themselves in crises on 'keeping their wits about them,'

[7] Eliot, *Japanese Buddhism*, p. 401.

the Japanese feel that a millstone has fallen from around their necks when they deliver themselves up to the ecstasy of their souls and forget the restraints self-watchfulness imposes. As we have seen, their culture dins the need for circumspection into their souls, and the Japanese have countered by declaring that there is a more efficient plane of human consciousness where this burden falls away.

The most extreme form in which the Japanese state this tenet, at least to the ears of an Occidental, is the way they supremely approve of the man 'who lives as already dead.' The literal Western translation would be 'the living corpse,' and in all Occidental languages 'the living corpse' is an expression of horror. It is the phrase by which we say that a man's self has died and left his body encumbering the earth. No vital principle is left in him. The Japanese use 'living as one already dead' to mean that one lives on the plane of 'expertness.' It is used in common everyday exhortation. To encourage a boy who is worrying about his final examinations from middle school, a man will say, 'Take them as one already dead and you will pass them easily.' To encourage someone who is undertaking an important business deal, a friend will say, 'Be as one already dead.' When a man goes through a great soul crisis and cannot see his way ahead, he quite commonly emerges with the resolve to live 'as one already dead.' . . .

The philosophy which underlies muga underlies also 'living as already dead.' In this state a man eliminates all self-watchfulness and thus all fear and circumspection. He becomes as the dead, who have passed beyond the necessity of taking thought about the proper course of action. The dead are no longer returning *on*; they are free. Therefore to say, 'I will live as one already dead' means a supreme release from conflict. It means, 'My energy and attention are free to pass directly to the fulfillment of my purpose. My observer-self with all its burden of fears is no longer between me and my goal. With it have gone the sense of tenseness and strain and the tendency toward depression that troubled my earlier strivings. Now all things are possible to me.'

In Western phraseology, the Japanese in the practice of muga and of 'living as one already dead' eliminate the conscience. What they call 'the observing-self,' 'the interfering self,' is a censor judging one's acts. It points up vividly the difference between Western and Eastern psychology that when we speak of a conscienceless American we mean a man who no longer feels the sense of sin which should accompany wrongdoing, but that when a Japanese uses the equivalent phrase he means a man who is no longer tense and hindered. The American means a bad man; the Japanese means a good man, a trained man, a man able to use his abilities to the utmost. He means a man who can perform the most difficult and devoted deeds of unselfishness. The great American sanction for good behavior is guilt; a man who because of a calloused conscience can no longer feel this has become antisocial. The Japanese diagram the problem differently. According to their philosophy man in his inmost soul is good. If his impulse can be directly embodied in his deed, he acts virtuously and easily. Therefore he undergoes, in 'expertness,' self-training to eliminate the self-censorship of shame (haji). Only then is his 'sixth sense' free of hindrance. It is his supreme release from self-consciousness and conflict. . . .

The Study of Cultural Patterns in European Nations

✤ Every nation in Europe and Asia has simultaneously denied and boasted that it had a national character. It has been almost impossible to separate the wheat from the chaff in the extravagant statements that have been put forth, and many social scientists have been inclined to chalk up the whole problem as a subject for popular oratory, and to throw it out of court as a matter for systematic investigation. During the war years, however, the problem of national character became a matter of grave practical importance. There were crucial questions as to "the nature of the enemy," the receptivity of satellite nations to certain kinds of appeals and not to others, and the opposition of certain of the allied nations to measures easily accepted by others. Those who were engaged in psychological warfare, in political conferences, in the training of OSS and UNRRA personnel, as well as those engaged in military operations, were constantly handicapped if they made mistakes in estimating the way a *vis-à-vis* nation would think and behave. It was of the utmost importance to

REPRINTED WITH PERMISSION of The New York Academy of Sciences from *Transactions*, ser. 2, 8:274–79 (1946).

eliminate popular fantasies and misapprehensions, and to use whatever techniques the social sciences could offer, in order to understand these national characters.

To the anthropologist, the study of national character is a study of learned cultural behavior. For several decades before the war, anthropologists had done pioneer work, in this field, in compact primitive communities. During the last decade, theoretical points made by anthropologists about cultural conditioning had been widely accepted. Anthropologists had presented their case convincingly enough so that there was wide agreement that social arrangements are of fundamental importance in shaping any people's tenets about life, whether they are assumptions about the function of the State, economic motivations, relations between the sexes, or dependence upon the supernatural. The forms these tenets take in our own cultural background were no longer generally considered to be direct consequences of human biology, and "human nature" was no longer considered as a sufficient explanation of them. Behavior, even in civilized nations, was increasingly understood as ways of acting and thinking which developed in the special kind of social environment characteristic of that part of the world.

In 1943, I was asked to join the Office of War Information, to work on national character in enemy and occupied countries. I was asked to use the insights and techniques anthropology had developed in the study of learned cultural behavior. In spite of all the necessary limitations imposed upon research in the social sciences during war, it was a great opportunity. Studies of modern society had very seldom, indeed, made systematic use of the methods upon which anthropologists had based their analyses of the simpler societies. These methods were quite specific, and were designed to investigate how each new generation had learned and transmitted its way of life in all its specificities. They were methods for detailed studies of specific social environments. Experience had shown that it was necessary to stress many aspects of life which rate as trivia in Western international studies. Habit formation in a specific social environment; the rewards and punishments bestowed by society; the praise allotted to certain kinds of achievement; the connotations given to exercise of authority, and to submission to it, in day-by-day living; the degree to which responsibility for his own conduct was entrusted to the individual—all such questions had been regarded as essential in cultural investigations of behavior in primitive societies, and had hardly been raised in studies of European nations. In classic studies of civilized countries, the approach is, ordinarily, either historical, or economic, or political. Though such segmented approaches are valuable and necessary, they still leave a wide field for applications of methods which have been successfully used in anthropological studies of learned cultural behavior.

In attempting, during the war, to use such techniques in the study of civilized nations, there was a grave handicap, occasioned not by the nature of the research, but by the fact of war. The anthropologist's chief technique, that of the field trip, was impossible. There were available, however, in the United States, persons of almost every nation of the world, and it was a fairly simple matter to find transplanted groups which retained a great deal of the way of life to which the older members had been born. Individuals could be found from most classes and minorities, and from most of the distinctive provinces of a nation. It was not necessary to give up the traditional anthropological reliance upon face-to-face study, and this recourse to informants was all the more necessary, the clearer it became that much essential material for the studies I had been asked to make was not elsewhere available.

The usual comment on such projected studies of civilized countries is that, quite apart from the limitations imposed by the war, civilized nations are too difficult to study by methods that may be sufficient in small communities. Such skepticism is often based on what should rather be regarded as a great advantage: the multiplicity of the facts known and recorded about Western nations. Actually, the anthropologist working on civilized nations has a great head-start, in that much work has been done in historical research; that statistics are available in many fields; that so many observers have recorded their personal experiences; that there are often excellent novels available; and that the language does not present the grave obstacles it does in tribes where it has never been recorded and ordered in grammatical categories. Vast quantities of material are a handicap only when the crucial problems to be investigated are not formulated. When they are, it is possible to cull the relevant material from the most diverse sources. The richness of the data is an asset, and, when lacunae were discovered, it was usually possible to obtain necessary facts from informants. The principal advantage the anthropologist had, was that certain ways of stating the problems had emerged from his experience, and stating the problem so that it can be answered by research is usually half the battle.

Skepticism about the application of anthropological techniques to civilized nations is also often based on the lack of cultural homogeneity in modern nations. This kind of skepticism frequently seems to the anthropologist to be no criticism of his method, but a statement of an elementary principle which he completely accepts. No anthropologist, I think, would attempt to study "the" character structure of such a welter of cultures as were included within the national boundaries of Yugoslavia. There are other multicultural states such as Poland and Czechoslovakia. Such conditions do not mean that investigation must be abandoned. The solution is to multiply the number of investigations to any desired point, and this holds true also of such lesser problems as are presented by the different regions of England, or of France, or of the United States.

The criticism that the degree of class differentiation prevalent in Western civilization makes the use of anthropological methods impossible, stands on a somewhat different footing. Adequate cultural study of this situation, including all the relevant factors, has hardly been attempted in Western nations. Such a study would investigate what attitudes and convictions the various classes have in common in any nation, as well as the obvious fact of conflict of interests. Even the conflict situation is usually inadequately stated. The trained anthropologist, in any study of complementary behavior, whether between authoritarian fathers and submissive sons, or between despotic kings and their subjects, has to present both parties as actors in a patterned situation. He can see it as a kind of see-saw, and by studying the height of the fulcrum and the length of the board (in the study of classes, laws about property and land, general conditions of social security, and the like), he can show either that the group on the high end of the see-saw is necessarily very far up and the group on the low end very far down, or that they are more nearly balanced. As extremes, material or psychological, are eliminated from one position, extremes will also be eliminated from the other. Other groups in the society, too, may throw their weight now to one party and now to the other. The anthropologist has good reason to know, also, that nonmaterial factors may be as important as material ones in any given situation, and he investigates, for instance, the cultural acceptance of hierarchy, as well as the relative frequency of wealth and poverty.

The similarity of the basic assumptions about life made by both those classes, in any nation, is of great importance. The wealthy industrialist and the laborer or peasant, in a nation or area of Western civilization, hold many attitudes in common. The attitude toward property only in part depends upon whether one is rich or whether one is poor. Property may be, as in Holland, something which is an almost inseparable part of one's own self-esteem, something to be added to, kept immaculately, and never spent carelessly. This is true, whether the individual belongs to court circles or can only say in the words of a proverbial expression: "If it's only a penny a year, lay it by." Alternatively, the attitude toward property may be quite different, as in Rumania. An upper-class person may be, or become, a pensioner of a wealthy man, without loss of status or self-confidence; his property, he says, is not "himself." And the poor peasant argues that, being poor, it is futile for him to lay anything by; "he would," he says, "if he were rich." The well-to-do increase their possessions by other means than thrift, and the traditional attitude toward property differences associates wealth with luck or exploitation, rather than with assured position as in Holland. In each of these countries, as in other European nations, many of which have deeply embedded special attitudes toward property, the specific nature of these assumptions can be greatly clarified by study of what is required of the child in his handling and ownership of property, and under what sanctions and conditions expanding opportunities are allowed in adolescence, and at his induction into fully adult status.

Attitudes toward authority are similarly localized. A Greek, whether he belongs to the upper classes, or whether he is a peasant villager, has a characteristic opposition to authority from above, which permeates daily conversation and influences his choice of a means of livelihood quite as much as it colors his political attitudes. On the other hand, it is quite true that, in other regions of Europe, in the dramatic words of Ortega y Gasset, there has been a "formidable cry rising like the howling of innumerable dogs asking for someone or something to take command, to impose an occupation, a duty." During the war, Goebbels's propaganda broadcasts quoted the well-known words of Machiavelli, saying that all Germans knew they were true: "Men work either under compulsion, or of their own will. The greatest energy they display where their own choice has the least freedom." Such authoritarianism deserves the closest cultural study. It requires knowledge, not only of the laws and of the economic set-up that have fostered it, but of the child's first experiences with authority, and of the sanctions which are invoked. It requires knowledge of the age at which various disciplines are imposed, and of the rewards of obedience. Such knowledge can lead directly to a clearer insight into what the leaders in any country are saying in their political speeches, and into what courses of action the people of that country can advantageously follow in reconstruction. Character structure can, of course, change over generations, as different experiences are provided, but the very process of change can be illuminated by systematic study of behavior in this generation.

At present, even the recorded facts necessary for a cultural study of the nations of Europe are widely scattered in different publications, and much crucial information is not recorded at all. Our understanding of international affairs is about where our understanding of primitive peoples was before the anthropologists attempted the serious study of how primitive people *learned* their cultural behavior. Even those students who have used the method in the simpler cultures have usually laid it aside when they came to discussions of our own civilization. They tend to assume a similarity in experience among the different Western nations, which my investigations showed did not exist. There are differences of the same order as those with which we are familiar in the isolated simpler cultures. We need studies of Western peoples which show them to us as people who have learned, in specific ways, to solve the universal human problems by special cultural arrangements to which they give their allegiance as we do to ours. We need intimate understanding of their experiences, so that we shall learn to discriminate between what is truly socially dangerous and what is only another method of arriving at a socially desirable goal. The kinds of strength which the people of each area could use in a world organized for peace can only be those to which they have been bred. If we insist that they imitate another kind of strength, they will be powerless to contribute. If we, the people of the world, are ever to achieve a world organization which promises mutual benefits, we must be scientifically prepared to know the strength which different nations of the world can utilize to this end.

Anthropology and the Humanities

✠ Anthropology belongs among the sciences in far more senses than the obvious one that it sits on the National Research Council and on the Social Science Research Council. From the moment of its professional beginnings just about a hundred years ago, it has phrased the problems it investigated and has adopted conceptual schemes according to patterns which belong to the scientific tradition of Western Civilization of the past century. It borrowed some of its early concepts, such as that of evolution or of the single localized origin of civilization, directly from phylogenetic concepts of biology, and it has attempted in all its serious work to arrive at objective, theoretical, generalized descriptions of reality.

This scientific framework in which anthropology has worked and developed has not prevented it from falling into error or from exploring blind alleys. Anthropology, like any science, must constantly rephrase its questions in the light of new discriminations in its own field and of new knowledge available to it in the work of other sciences. It must constantly try to profit by methods and concepts which have been developed in the physical and biological sciences, in psychology and in psychiatry. In this present decade we have every opportunity to do so; we are no longer living in an age which concerns itself with controversies about how to delimit and to define each self-sufficient science.

The situation is quite different in regard to anthropology and the humanities. They are so far apart that it is still quite possible to ignore even the fact that they deal with the same subject matter—man and his works and his ideas and his history. To my mind the very nature of the problems posed and discussed in the humanities is closer, chapter by chapter,

Address of the Retiring President of the American Anthropological Association, Albuquerque, New Mexico, December, 1947.

Reprinted with permission of the American Anthropological Association from *American Anthropologist* 50:585–93 (1948).

to those in anthropology than are the investigations carried on in most of the social sciences. This is a heretical statement and to justify it I must turn back to the great days of the humanities.

From the Renaissance down to a hundred years ago, the humanities, not the sciences, were the intellectual food of Western civilization. *Humanitas* meant then, as it meant to Cicero, the knowledge of what man is—his powers, his relations to his fellows and to nature, and the knowledge of the limits of these human powers and of man's responsibility. It was in this field of the Study of Man that, after the Renaissance, methods of impartial inquiry were developed. As President Conant has recently written: [1]

> *In the first period of the Renaissance the love of dispassionate search for the truth was carried forward by those who were concerned with man and his works rather than with inanimate or animate nature. It was the humanist's exploration of antiquity that came nearest to exemplifying our modern ideas of impartial inquiry.*

One has only to read some of Montaigne's essays written in the sixteenth century to realize their kinship to modern anthropology. Montaigne, the humanist, in his accounts of his conversations with his Tupinamba servant, could discuss the economics of daily life and the torture and eating of captives in this great South American tribe from the point of view of his "boy" who had grown up there; the great Frenchman did not apply to the Tupinamba the categories of Western European, Catholic, and French morals and economics. Like any modern anthropological field worker, he used an informant and compared cultures without weighting his argument in favor of his own ethnocentric attitudes. However slight the attempt he made in the primitive field, it belongs in the modern anthropological tradition.

This general statement of the common subject matter of the humanities and of anthropology still does not do justice to their likenesses. The humanities provided Europeans of that period with experience in cultures other than their own. Because Greece and Rome were the prime inspira-

[1] James B. Conant, *On Understanding Science* (New Haven: Yale University Press, 1947), pp. 8–9.

tion of the Renaissance, learning tended to be justified by the freedom it gave the scholar to move intellectually in a culture different from the one in which he had been reared. The humanities, in consequence, were an intense cross-cultural experience, and their aims were often couched in the same phrases as those of modern anthropological investigation of an alien culture.

Renaissance classical studies often became, as is always only too likely, authoritarian and formal, but for discerning scholars from Erasmus to John Stuart Mill their purpose was still to provide enlightenment by the study of another culture. Mill put his pleas for the study of the humanities, organized as they were around Greek and Latin literature, in exactly these terms.

> *Without knowing . . . some people other than ourselves, we remain, to the hour of our death, with our intellects only half expanded; . . . we cannot divest ourselves of preconceived notions. There is no means of eliminating their influence but by frequently using the differently colored glasses of other people; and those of other nations, as the most different, are the best.*

It was in this field of the humanities that great men for centuries got their cross-cultural insights. It liberated them, it taught them discipline of mind. It dominated the intellectual life of the period. Then about the middle of the last century the new sciences began to take leadership out of the hands of the humanists. Until then science had hardly got a foothold in the colleges and universities, and it had remained largely a field for amateurs. Its subject matter for generations had been suspect, not only because scientists had questioned facts upheld by contemporary religion, but because the natural sciences dealt with matter and inanimate nature, which stood low in the divine order of the world. They were regarded as enemies of man's higher interests, which were the peculiar field of the humanities.

Professional anthropology had its beginnings during the years which at last recognized in the sciences, at least potentially, the place they have come to hold in Western civilization. The excitement of phrasing the study of man in terms of scientific generalizations instead of in humanistic terms was basic in the whole discipline of anthropology. There were great gains in this new phrasing. But, looking back at it now, there were also losses. Such a great prescientific compilation as that done by Sahagun among the Aztecs was not duplicated by professional anthropologists of the age of Ratzel and Tylor. Instead Spencer collected his huge scrapbooks of meager travelers' items from the five continents and the islands of the seas, and Morgan found it possible to classify his kinship terminologies without ethnological investigation of the significance of the actual relation to forms of marriage or of localized and nonlocalized residence of kin. Professional anthropologists of this period did not engage in conversations such as those of Montaigne with his Tupinamba boy; they studied marriage or religion or magic in the British Museum without benefit of any informant. William James reports that when he asked Frazer about natives he had known, Frazer exclaimed, "But Heaven forbid!"

With all this in mind, it is tempting to imagine what struggles need never have occurred in later anthropological work and theory if anthropology had originally become a professional study before that turning point in the nineteenth century when the sciences came to dominate the field of intellectual inquiry. It is easy to imagine that anthropology might have then stemmed from and continued the methods and insights of the humanities.

No one is more convinced than I am that anthropology has profited by being born within the scientific tradition. The humanist tradition did not construct hypotheses about man's cultural life which it then proceeded to test by cross-cultural study; such procedure belongs in the scientific tradition. My conviction is simply that today the scientific and humanist traditions are not opposites nor mutually exclusive. They are supplementary, and modern anthropology handicaps itself in method and insight by neglecting the work of the great humanists.

In the early days of anthropology a great gulf divided it from the humanities. As a young scientific discipline anthropology sought to formulate generalizations about social evolution which would parallel biology's phylogenetic tree, or about the psychic unity of man and the vast repetitiousness of his behavior. The basic and unverbalized assumption was that human culture could be reduced to order by the same kind of concepts which had proved useful in the nonhuman world.

This was a reasonable expectation, and those who sought to realize it had good reason to leave out of account any consideration of human emotion, ethics, rational insight and purpose which had come into being within man's social life. They abstracted, instead, categories of institutions, ranged from the simple to the complex, and discussed them as if they were species in the world of nature. They lifted items of human magic and kinship like blocks out of the cultural edifices where these materials had been relevant in native life, and classified them as a botanist of the time classified the flowers. Even today, when most anthropologists define culture so that it includes human attitudes and behavior, there are some who still exclude the mind and purposes of man, and, indeed, a "science of culturology" and certain kinds of historical reconstruction and of cultural cycles are at present only possible if this exclusion has been made.

The great majority of present-day American anthropologists, however, include the mind of man within their definition of culture—man's emotions, his rationalizations, his symbolic structures. Such anthropologists' theoretical interests have moved strongly in the direction of trying to understand the relation of man himself to his cultural constructs. They have moved in this direction often as a consequence of the vivid material available in this field in anthropological field work, whether their own or others', and they have often not considered sufficiently the difference in training which genuine progress in this field requires.

For if anthropology studies the mind of man, along with his institutions, our greatest resource, it seems to me, is the humanities. By this I mean not all contemporary literary criticism and all contemporary history, but those surviving humanists who are still genuinely in the humanistic tradition. History, literary criticism or classical studies can be written in the humanistic tradition or in the scientific. Scientific method has had unparalleled prestige in the last hundred years, and the humanities, no less than anthropology, have often and sometimes profitably taken over methods of science.

The great tradition of the humanities, from the Renaissance to the present day, is distinguished by command of vast detail about men's thinking and acting in different periods and places, and the sensitivities it has consequently fostered to the quality of men's minds and emotions. History, as a humanitarian art, left out vital economic and political analyses, but it did try to show the deeds and aims of men in a certain period and what the consequences of these were; it might picture men's deeds as vagaries or as destructive but it tied them with consequences; it pictured man as responsible for his successes and his failures. Literary criticism might raise the problem of the spirit of the age or confine itself to the character of one hero; in either case, it was concerned to show that, given certain specific kinds of emotion or of thought, people would act in given ways and the denouement would be of a given sort. The humanities have based their work on the premise of man's creativity and of the consequences of his acts and thoughts in his own world. Their methods of study have been consistent with their premises.

Both method and premise differ from those which have proved valuable in the field of natural science. There the student has to analyze the world of nature, which, as we know, can be described by determinate laws. He has only to find out the law of a falling body or of an expanding gas and he can apply the formula in any context. He can even make large generalizations about animals, since they are not biologically specialized to learn and invent. But man is a species which can create his way of life—his culture. He is not for this reason outside the natural order; rather, natural evolution has, in man, produced an animal who is not merely a creature of circumstance and of instincts but an initiator and inventor. His social life has developed, for good or evil, within a human framework of purposes which he has himself invented and espoused, and the course of evolution, at this human stage, has therefore taken on characteristics which are not present at the prehuman stage. Man is a creature with such freedom of action and of imagination that he can, for instance, by not accepting a trait, prevent the occurrence of diffusion, or he can at any stage of technological development create his gods in the most diverse form. Even granted that many correlations, such as that between technological stage and the character of supernatural beings, have high probability, it is only to the degree that we know concrete and detailed facts about any people—their contacts with other tribes, their location in a cultural area—that we can assume the correlations to hold.

The gradual recognition of these facts has led anthropologists to include the mind of man within their definition of culture. The nature of this anthropological problem has inevitably shown them the common ground they have with psychology and psychiatry. By the same necessity, if they are to interpret their data adequately, they will increasingly find common ground with the great humanists. It is my thesis that we can analyze cultural attitudes and behavior more cogently if we know Santayana's *Three Philosophical Poets* and Lovejoy's *Great Chain of Being* and the great works of Shakespearian criticism. Future anthropological work, too, can reach a higher level if we attract, not only students of sociology, but also students of the humanities. I shall assume that we might better learn from the great masters than from the lesser and I shall try to illustrate what I believe they have to offer.

Santayana, certainly one of the greatest of living humanists, has written in almost all the fields of cultural anthropology. He has not dealt with primitive material, but whether his subject is Greek or Hebrew civilization, or English as in *Soliloquies in England,* or our own as in *Character and Opinion in the United States,* he has dealt with the ways of life men have embodied in their cultures, the institutions in which they have expressed them, and the kinds of emotion and of ideas which have taken root in men so reared. He has constantly illustrated from the side of the humanities and out of his own cultivated sensitivity the truth about culture which he has phrased in one of his books published twenty years ago: [2]

> *Any world, any society, any language . . . satisfies and encourages the spirit which it creates. It fits the imagination because it has kindled and molded it, and it satisfies its resident passions because these are such, and such only, as could take root and become habitual in precisely that world. This natural harmony between the spirit and its conditions is the only actual one; it is the source of every ideal and the sole justification of any hope. Imperfect and shifting as this harmony must be, it is sufficient to support the spirit of man.*

[2] George Santayana, *Platonism and the Spiritual Life* (New York: Scribner's, 1927), p. 58.

This fine summary of the interdependence of man's cultural institutions and of the personalities of those who live within the realm of their influence is one of Santayana's great themes. He brought all his learning and philosophy to bear against the position, so common among social scientists who were his contemporaries, that a fundamental opposition existed between society and the individual, and that to show man's debt to his cultural tradition was to minimize his claim to originality and free will. Whether Santayana was discussing great artists or great religious masters, his thesis was the same: only those "can show great originality [who] are trained in distinct and established schools; for originality and genius must be largely fed and raised on the shoulders of some old tradition." [3] The worst conditions for cross-cultural understanding, according to Santayana, are present among those who throw over all they regard as established tradition; the best, among those who respect their own canons and dogmas; no matter how dissimilar their beliefs, they have a common ground, and they can best understand each other. When the modern anthropologist says that in any cross-cultural work it is better for the student to be sure of his own ethnic and national position and loyalties, he is echoing Santayana's point, and he can profit by his wisdom.

Santayana's volumes also deal with the topical subject matter of anthropology: social organization, religion, art, and speculative thought. He saw all these arts of man as rooted in the culture of a given time and place. His analysis of Greece and that of the Hebrews, and of the growth of Christianity in Europe, was a part of his *Reason in Religion* which was published in 1905. It is still to my mind indispensable to any anthropologist who is studying religion, and there is no better illustration of the deeper insight the methods of the humanities had achieved than a comparison of *Reason in Religion* with Tylor's *Primitive Culture*—and *Primitive Culture* is a favorite book on my shelves. Tylor performed well the task he set himself, but the humanist's approach to his problem, being holistic and always taking account of context in the mind of man, allows him to investigate problems which have not yet been adequately treated from anthropological material.

In Santayana's *Three Philosophical Poets*, too, he is studying three con-

[3] George Santayana, *The Life of Reason*, 2 vols. (New York, Scribner's, 1905–1906), 2:101.

trasting cultures, those represented by Lucretius, by Dante, and by Goethe. He is concerned to characterize the "cosmic parables" of these three poets as different ways of viewing life, different ways of conceiving man's fate. They are contrasted studies of the genius of three great civilizations, and I think no anthropologist can read them without profit.

I have stressed Santayana's humanistic studies of culture, but the humanities—even as exemplified in Santayana—do not necessarily deal with culture. Shakespearian criticism is a case in point, and it has nevertheless been most valuable to me as an anthropologist. Long before I knew anything at all about anthropology, I had learned from Shakespearian criticism—and from Santayana—habits of mind which at length made me an anthropologist.

I had learned, for example, from Furness' great Variorum editions, how drastically men's values and judgments are culturally conditioned. The stage versions of Shakespeare's plays rewritten in the eighteenth and nineteenth centuries reflected the temper of the age of Queen Anne, of the Georges, and of the Victorian era. Even the questions critics had asked about the characters in the plays were documentation on the age in which they were writing; for nearly two centuries after *Hamlet* became a favorite play on the London stage it did not occur to any one of them that there was anything particularly interesting in Hamlet's character. With the rise of romanticism this became the central interest of all commentators, and the most bizarre "explanations" were offered.

It was A. C. Bradley who, in his *Shakespearian Tragedy*, first published in 1904, cut his way through this underbrush and emphasized valid humanistic standards of criticism as applied, not only to the character of Hamlet, but of Iago and Macbeth and King Lear and other famous men and women of the tragedies. The core of his method was the critic's surrender to the text itself; he ruled out those "explanations" which sounded plausibly only so long as one did not remember the text. Shakespeare was, for Bradley, a dramatist able to set forth his characters with sufficient truth and completeness so that they would reveal themselves to the student who weighed carefully both what was said and what was not said, what was done and what was not done. In the worlds which Shakespeare portrayed, Bradley said, "We watch *what is*, seeing that so it happened and must have happened."

Bradley's canons of good Shakespearian criticism, and his practice of it, are as good examples of fruitful methods and high standards as a student of culture can desire. The anthropologist will, of course, use these canons for the study of a cultural ethos, and not for the elucidation of a single character, but he, like Bradley, knows that he will succeed in his work if he takes into account whatever is said and done, discarding nothing he sees to be relevant; if he tries to understand the interrelations of discrete bits; if he surrenders himself to his data and uses all the insights of which he is capable.

The anthropologist has still more to learn from such literary criticism as that of Bradley. For more than a decade anthropologists have agreed upon the value of the life history. Some have said that it was the essential tool in the study of a culture. Many life histories have been collected—many more than have been published. Very little, however, has been done even with those which are published, and field workers who collected them have most often merely extracted in their topical monographs bits about marriage or ceremonies or livelihood which they obtained in life histories. The nature of the life-history material made this largely inevitable, for I think anyone who has read great numbers of these autobiographies, published and unpublished, will agree that from eighty to ninety-five per cent of most of them are straight ethnographic reporting of culture. It is a time-consuming and repetitious way of obtaining straight ethnography, and if that is all they are to be used for, any field worker knows how to obtain such data more economically. The unique value of life histories lies in that fraction of the material which shows what repercussions the experiences of a man's life—either shared or idiosyncratic—have upon him as a human being molded in that environment. Such information, as it were, tests out a culture by showing its workings in the life of a carrier of that culture; we can watch in an individual case, in Bradley's words, "*what is*, seeing that so it happened and must have happened." But if we are to make our collected life histories count in anthropological theory and understanding, we have only one recourse: we must be willing and able to study them according to the best tradition of the humanities. None of the social sciences, not even psychology, has adequate models for such studies. The humanities have. If we are to use life histories for more than items of topical ethnology, we shall have to be willing to do the kind of job on them which has traditionally been done by the great humanists.

Shakespearian criticism has pressed on in recent years in several new directions which are instructive to the anthropologist. Bradley wrote before the days of modern detailed research into Elizabethan beliefs, events, and stage practices. This is true cultural study in the humanitarian tradition, and all such knowledge is essential for an understanding of Shakespeare's plays. Such research compares, for instance, pirated texts in the early quartos with the texts of the folio collected edition; it studies the diaries and papers of a great Elizabethan theater owner in order to reconstruct the conditions under which the plays were produced. More than all, it describes the current ideas of Shakespearian times in science, history, morals, and religion, both those accepted by the "groundlings" and those aired among the elite. As Dover Wilson has shown in his critical edition of *Hamlet*, such a cultural study is crucial. Only with a knowledge of what the current ideas were about ghosts and their communications with their descendants can one judge what Shakespeare was saying in *Hamlet*; one can understand Hamlet's relations with his mother only with an acquaintance with what incest was in Elizabethan times, and what it meant to contract an "o'erhasty marriage" where "the funeral baked meats did coldly furnish forth the marriage tables."

Carolyn Spurgeon's and Dr. Armstrong's examination of Shakespeare's imagery is another kind of study from which an anthropologist can learn a technique useful in the study of comparative cultures. It can reveal symbolisms and free associations which fall into patterns and show processes congenial to the human mind in different cultures.

In all that I have said, I have emphasized the common ground which is shared by the humanities and by anthropology so soon as it includes the mind and behavior of men in its definition of culture. I could have spoken about what anthropology in its present state of knowledge has to offer to the humanities, but that subject would not be crucial in a talk to anthropologists. It is important, however, for us to be aware of what we can learn from the humanities. Let me emphasize again that the humanities provide only some of the answers to our problems in cultural studies; there are problems in the comparative study of societies with which they do not deal. Because anthropology, as a social science, organized its work to arrive at certain generalized, theoretical statements about culture, it has been able to make and document certain points in the Study of Man which the humanities did not make.

My point is that, once anthropologists include the mind of man in their subject matter, the methods of science and the methods of the humanities complement each other. Any commitment to methods which exclude either approach is self-defeating. The humanists criticize the social sciences because they belabor the obvious and are arid; the social scientists criticize the humanities because they are subjective. It is not necessary for the anthropologist to be afraid of either criticism, neither of belaboring the obvious, nor of being subjective. The anthropologist can use both approaches. The adequate study of culture, our own and those on the opposite side of the globe, can press on to fulfillment only as we learn today from the humanities as well as from the sciences.

Selected Bibliography of the Writings of Ruth Benedict

(1917) 1959 * Mary Wollstonecraft. In *An Anthropologist at Work: Writings of Ruth Benedict*, by Margaret Mead, pp. 491–519. Boston: Houghton Mifflin.

1922 The Vision in Plains Culture. *American Anthropologist* 24:1–23. Reprinted in *An Anthropologist at Work*, pp. 18–35.

1923a The Concept of the Guardian Spirit in North America. *Memoirs of the American Anthropological Association* 29:1–97.

1923b A Matter for the Field Worker in Folk-Lore. *Journal of American Folk-Lore* 36:104. Reprinted in *An Anthropologist at Work*, pp. 36–37.

1924 A Brief Sketch of Serrano Culture. *American Anthropologist* 26:366–92. Reprinted (abridged) in *An Anthropologist at Work*, pp. 213–21.

(c.1925a) 1959 Counters in the Game. In *An Anthropologist at Work*, pp. 40–43.

(c.1925b) 1959 The Uses of Cannibalism. In *An Anthropologist at Work*, pp. 44–48.

1926 Serrano Tales. *Journal of American Folk-Lore* 39:1–17.

1928a Eucharist, by Anne Singleton (pseud.). *Nation* 127 (September 26):296. Reprinted in Selected Poems: 1941, in *An Anthropologist at Work*, p. 479. Reproduced in this volume, p. 75.

1928b Review of *L'Ame Primitive*, by Lucien Lévy-Bruhl. *Journal of Philosophy* 25:717–19.

1929 The Science of Custom. *Century Magazine* 117:641–49.

1930a Animism. In *Encyclopedia of the Social Sciences* 2:65–67. Edited by Edwin R. A. Seligman and others, 15 volumes. New York: Macmillan.

* IN ORDER to preserve the chronological order, the date of composition of articles that were published posthumously is given first in parenthesis followed by the publication date.

Selected Bibliography

1930b Child Marriage. In *Encyclopedia of the Social Sciences* 3:395–97.

1930c Eight Stories from Acoma. *Journal of American Folk-Lore* 43:59–87.

1930d Psychological Types in the Cultures of the Southwest. In *Proceedings of the Twenty-third International Congress of Americanists, September 1928*, pp. 572–81. New York. Reprinted in *An Anthropologist at Work*, pp. 248–61.

1930e Review of *Der Ursprung der Gottesidee; Teil 2 Die Religionen der Urvölker; Band 2 Die Religionen der Urvölker Amerikas*, by Wilhelm Schmidt, S. V. D. *Journal of American Folk-Lore* 43:444–45.

1931a Dress. In *Encyclopedia of the Social Sciences* 5:235–37.

1931b Folklore. In *Encyclopedia of the Social Sciences* 6:288–93.

1931c Tales of the Cochiti Indians. *Bureau of American Ethnology Bulletin* No. 98. Washington.

1932a Configurations of Culture in North America. *American Anthropologist* 34:1–27. Reproduced in this volume, pp. 80–105.

1932b Review of *Eskimo*, by Peter Freuchen. *American Anthropologist* 34:720–21.

1932c Review of *Ethical Relativity*, by Edward Westermarck. *Books* (*New York Herald Tribune* weekly book review), August 6.

1933a Magic. In *Encyclopedia of the Social Sciences* 10:39–44. Reproduced (abridged) in this volume, pp. 105–15.

1933b Myth. In *Encyclopedia of the Social Sciences* 11:178–81.

1934a Anthropology and the Abnormal. *Journal of General Psychology* 10:59–82. Reprinted in *An Anthropologist at Work*, pp. 262–83.

1934b *Patterns of Culture*. Boston: Houghton Mifflin.

1934c Ritual. In *Encyclopedia of the Social Sciences* 13:396–98.

1935a *Zuni Mythology*, 2 vols. Columbia University Contributions to Anthropology, No. 21. New York: Columbia University Press. Reprinted 1969, New York: AMS Press. Introduction (abridged) reproduced in this volume, pp. 115–34.

1935b Review of *Sex and Culture*, by J. D. Unwin. *American Anthropologist* 37:691–92.

1936a Marital Property Rights in Bilateral Society. *American Anthropologist* 38:368–73.

1936b Review of *Manus Religion*, by Reo F. Fortune. *Review of Religion* 1:48–50.

1937a Review of *Chan Kom: A Maya Village*, by Robert Redfield and Alfonso Villa R. *American Anthropologist* 39:340–42.

1937b Review of *Naven*, by Gregory Bateson. *Review of Religion* 2:63–66.

1938a Continuities and Discontinuities in Cultural Conditioning. *Psychiatry* 1:161–67.

1938b Religion. In *General Anthropology*, ed. Franz Boas, pp. 627–65. Boston and New York: Heath.

1938c Review of *Die Frau im öffentlichen Leben in Melanesien,* by Joachim Henning. *American Anthropologist* 40:163.

1938d Review of *The Neurotic Personality of Our Time,* by Karen Horney. *Journal of Social and Abnormal Psychology* 33:133–35.

1939a Edward Sapir. *American Anthropologist* 41:465–77.

(1939b) 1959 The Natural History of War. In *An Anthropologist at Work,* pp. 369–82.

1940a Alexander Goldenweiser. *Modern Quarterly* 11:32–33.

1940b *Race: Science and Politics.* New York: Viking. Rev. ed. reprinted 1959, together with *The Races of Mankind,* by Ruth Benedict and Gene Weltfish, New York: Viking.

1940c Review of *Pueblo Indian Religion,* by Elsie Clews Parsons. *Review of Religion* 4:438–40.

1941a Our Last Minority: Youth. *New Republic* 105:279–80.

(c.1941b) 1959 Ideologies in the Light of Comparative Data. Excerpt in *An Anthropologist at Work,* pp. 383–85.

1941c Privileged Classes: An Anthropological Problem. *Frontiers of Democracy* 7:110–12.

1941d Race Problems in America. *Annals,* The American Academy of Political and Social Sciences 216:73–78.

1941e Review of *Pascua: A Yaqui Village in Arizona,* by Edward H. Spicer. *American Historical Review* 47:170–71.

(c.1942a) 1959 The Bond of Fellowship. In *An Anthropologist at Work,* pp. 356–57.

1942b Primitive Freedom. *Atlantic Monthly* 169:756–63. Reprinted in *An Anthropologist at Work,* pp. 386–98. Reproduced in this volume, pp. 134–46.

1942c Review of *An Apache Way of Life,* by Morris E. Opler. *American Anthropologist* 44:692–93.

1942d Review of *Becoming a Kwoma,* by John M. Whiting. *Journal of Social and Abnormal Psychology* 37:409–10.

1942e Review of *Escape from Freedom,* by Erich Fromm. *Psychiatry* 5:111–13.

1942f Review of *Principles of Anthropology,* by E. D. Chapple and C. S. Coon. *Psychiatry* 5:450–51.

1943a Franz Boas as an Ethnologist. In *Franz Boas, 1858–1942,* pp. 27–34. Memoirs of the American Anthropological Association, No. 61.

1943b Human Nature Is Not a Trap. *Partisan Review* 10:159–64.

1943c Recognition of Cultural Diversities in the Postwar World. *Annals,* The American Academy of Political and Social Sciences 228:101–7. Reprinted in *An Anthropologist at Work,* pp. 439–48.

(1943d) 1972 *Rumanian Culture and Behavior.* Occasional Papers on Anthropology, No.

Selected Bibliography

1. Anthropology Club and Anthropology Faculty, Colorado State University (Fort Collins, Colorado).

(1943e) 1952 *Thai Culture and Behavior: An Unpublished War Time Study Dated September, 1943.* Data Paper No. 4, Southeast Asia Program, Department of Far Eastern Studies, Cornell University.

1943f Two Patterns of Indian Acculturation. *American Anthropologist* 45:207–12.

1943g (With Gene Weltfish) *The Races of Mankind.* Public Affairs Pamphlet No. 85. New York: Public Affairs Committee. Reprinted 1959, together with *Race: Science and Politics*, rev. ed., by Ruth Benedict, New York: Viking.

1946a *The Chrysanthemum and the Sword: Patterns of Japanese Culture.* Boston: Houghton Mifflin. Chapter 11 (abridged) reproduced in this volume, pp. 146–59.

(1946b) 1959 Remarks on Receiving the Annual Achievement Award of the American Association of University Women. Abridged in *An Anthropologist at Work*, pp. 430–32, and reproduced in this volume, pp. 66–68.

1946c The Study of Cultural Patterns in European Nations. *Transactions*, The New York Academy of Sciences, Ser. 2, 8:274–79. Reproduced in this volume, pp. 159–65.

(1947a) 1959 Postwar Race Prejudice. In *An Anthropologist at Work*, pp. 361–68.

1947b Review of *The Road of Life and Death: A Ritual Drama of the American Indians*, by Paul Radin. *American Anthropologist* 49:282–83.

1948 Anthropology and the Humanities. *American Anthropologist* 50:585–93. Reprinted in *An Anthropologist at Work*, pp. 459–70. Reproduced in this volume, pp. 165–76.

1949a Child Rearing in Certain European Countries. *American Journal of Orthopsychiatry* 19:342–48. Reprinted in *An Anthropologist at Work*, pp. 449–58.

1949b The Family: Genus americanum. In *The Family: Its Function and Destiny*, ed. Ruth Nanda Anshen, pp. 159–66. New York: Harper.

1949c Myth. In *Ruth Fulton Benedict: A Memorial*, p. 20. New York: Viking Fund. Reprinted in Selected Poems: 1941, in *An Anthropologist at Work*, p. 477. Reproduced in this volume, p. 24.

1950 The Study of Cultural Continuities, and An Outline for Research on Child Training in Different Cultures. In *Towards World Understanding*, 6. *The Influence of Home and Community on Children under Thirteen Years of Age*, pp. 5–13, 15–25. Paris: UNESCO.

1956 The Growth of Culture. In *Man, Culture, and Society*, ed. Harry L. Shapiro, pp. 182–95. New York: Oxford University Press.